Nurturing NEURO-DIVERSITY

Creative Strategies for Engaging Young Learners

Sarah Taylor Vanover, EdD

I0806395

Gryphon House

Published by Gryphon House, Inc.
P. O. Box 10, Lewisville, NC 27023
800.638.0928; 877.638.7576 [fax]

Visit us on the web at www.gryphonhouse.com.

Library of Congress Control Number: 2025930343

BULK PURCHASE

Gryphon House books are available for special premiums and sales promotions as well as for fund-raising use. Special editions or book excerpts can also be created to specifications. For details, call 800.638.0928.

DISCLAIMER

Gryphon House, Inc., cannot be held responsible for damage, mishap, or injury incurred during the use of or because of activities in this book. Appropriate and reasonable caution and adult supervision of children involved in activities and corresponding to the age and capability of each child involved are recommended at all times. Do not leave children unattended at any time. Observe safety and caution at all times.

Dedication

This book is dedicated to Abby Whitaker, Melanie Biggs, Jamie Harvener, Maggie Gregory, Kaylee Monroe, Melissa Goble, Laurie Fields, and all the amazing dance instructors who have patiently supported my son to be the best dancer (and best person) he can be! Thank you doesn't seem like enough!

TABLE OF CONTENTS

Preface: Robbie's Story

Unlike many children with an autism diagnosis, my son was not diagnosed until after he began elementary school. I think it is because he didn't have some of those stereotypical traits that many people expect to see with autism. Even as a very young child, he could make eye contact with people who were close to him, and he had an exceptional vocabulary. He didn't even line up all of his cars in a line and sort them by color. What people don't realize is that autism looks different on every child, so some of the typical red flags didn't really apply to him.

He went to a high-quality child-care program that allowed him to choose whether he wanted to participate in certain activities (such as circle time). He could be in social settings when he needed to be, but he often chose to play alone, depending on how loud and energetic the other children in the classroom were. At three and four years old, he seemed to be an independent but stubborn child who was a little shy around his peers. He was a picky eater, and he stopped taking a nap at school when he was sixteen months old. He wore a baseball cap to school every day, and he looked adorable in it. He was not a morning person, so it took him a while to warm up to the other children when he arrived at school. I was aware of his challenges, but they all seemed relatively appropriate for his age.

I did begin to get nervous as Robbie approached kindergarten. Preschool had allowed him to decline activities he didn't want to participate in, but elementary school would not be so forgiving. I also knew that he would have to begin schoolwork each morning when he arrived at school, instead of having a large amount of time to adjust to a structured school day. Since I already had an older son enrolled in our elementary school, I reached out to the school guidance counselor in advance to let her know that I was a little nervous, but like many other kindergarten parents before me, she reassured me that Robbie would adjust to his new surroundings once he had a couple of weeks to learn his new routine and feel comfortable with his new teachers. I know this conversation had served her well on so many other occasions, but it was not accurate for Robbie.

The structure of kindergarten caused Robbie to have multiple meltdowns per day when it was time to transition to a new activity before he was ready to do so. Leaving the classroom for music or art class was difficult for him, and the sensory overload of the cafeteria made Robbie dread lunchtime. When Robbie became overwhelmed, he would go into fight-or-flight mode. At school, he often chose flight. He would try to escape from whatever was causing him stress at the time. To avoid him fleeing from the classroom, the teacher set up an area by her desk where Robbie could retreat and try to calm himself down. He was allowed to bring comforting items to school and place them in a bag that he could get out when he needed to soothe himself.

A classroom full of twenty-five kindergarteners within a school of 700 elementary-school students also seemed to be overwhelming to Robbie at best. At home, we began to notice that Robbie was either emotionally exhausted each night or highly agitated. It was as if he had used all of his energy to hold himself together at school all day long, and once he got home, he couldn't manage it any longer. When he was awake and calm, he started showing odd behaviors that seemed to be calming him down, such as bouncing on the couch in a certain pattern over and over.

At school, Robbie wasn't interacting with the other children that often. When I asked, he told me that he didn't have any friends. He felt a strong connection with his teachers, but it still took a few weeks before he felt comfortable talking to them. The teacher said that he seemed to orient himself in the classroom in relation to where the teacher or the assistant teacher was at the time. He didn't seem as though he wanted to be with any particular classmates.

As I began to have more concerns about Robbie's behavior, I continued to mention it to the teacher and the school guidance counselor. The guidance counselor told me not to worry because Robbie was doing well on all of his schoolwork; she said it was just harder for him to adjust to the new school than some of the other students. She also noted that Robbie's test scores were high for his age and that many children classified as "gifted" often had many of the same struggles as Robbie. When I talked to the teacher, she seemed to have many of the same concerns that I did, but she told me that she didn't think there were specific services that the school could offer, since his academic work did not seem to be affected by his behavior.

Since the school seemed unable to provide answers, I started looking for specialists outside of the school who could help Robbie. He was becoming more aggressive at home in the evenings when he seemed overwhelmed, which was the behavior that was bothering me most. The pediatrician found it hard to believe that Robbie was hitting and biting me when he became upset; nevertheless, he recommended a counselor who specialized in working with young children. When I initially took Robbie to the counselor, I was expecting her to diagnose him with oppositional defiant disorder or something that focused on the aggression. I brought her detailed notes of all the behaviors that I had witnessed and been worried about for months. After our first visit, she told me that Robbie seemed to have high levels of anxiety, which could easily be the root of the fight-or-flight behaviors that we had witnessed, but she also said that she saw many behaviors that suggested Robbie might be on the autism spectrum.

This really took me by surprise. I thought I had a shy, stubborn child who did not like to follow directions. I viewed autism spectrum disorder as a disability that prohibited children from having social relationships with others, but Robbie and I had a close relationship (even though his emotions were not under control at times). Despite my lack of understanding at the time, I followed the counselor's advice and attempted to get him on several waitlists for a developmental evaluation. When I went back to the school with the information the counselor had given me, the school's staff seemed to think that her findings were inaccurate. The guidance counselor said she could agree with the anxiety evaluation, but she did not think Robbie fit the profile of a child with autism.

The disagreement of multiple professionals sent me on a deep dive for information about autism spectrum disorder. I knew that autism could look different from child to child, but I still had a distinct picture in my head of what I thought it included. As I learned more, I realized how Robbie's struggles with changes in routines and expectations were some of the key aspects of a possible autism diagnosis. He could not process large emotions, which often led to meltdowns or aggression. He was still spending most of his time at school by himself instead of starting new friendships. He continued to exhibit some of those repetitive behaviors each evening to calm himself down in his free time. He did not like to be in chaotic settings, at school or in the community. He ate a limited number of different foods, and he had a difficult time sleeping at night. I even learned that many children with autism also have a codiagnosis of anxiety, since they struggle so much with being in social settings and not knowing what to expect when they don't have an established routine.

By the time we were finally able to see a child psychologist and receive a diagnosis, I had already processed the fact that Robbie would most likely be diagnosed with autism spectrum disorder. It took until the end of first grade to finally get the results of all the medical evaluations that I had pursued for Robbie. He received a diagnosis of level 1 autism and generalized anxiety disorder. Once his diagnosis was established, I had to figure out how to get him the best support possible. He was already seeing a counselor after school, but I had to consider what type of therapy and education supports he might need. At that point, the COVID-19 pandemic had begun, and I was fighting to get him an individualized education program (IEP) during virtual learning.

For Robbie, virtual school was a dream come true. He was in our home all day long without having to leave and go to unfamiliar settings. He did not have to cope with a classroom of loud and energetic peers. He could eat the foods we provided at home, instead of school lunches, and when he was overwhelmed, he could retreat to his own bedroom.

Unfortunately, virtual learning did not address any of the social and emotional behavior goals that Robbie needed to work toward. A weekly Zoom meeting with the school behavioral therapist was not helping him develop relationships with peers or identify the emotions of others. With additional free time during the day, he was spending much more time on those repetitive behaviors, such as jumping on the couch. Also, the news and class discussions about the pandemic were causing his anxiety to increase. When his anxiety increased, he had more meltdowns from not having the skills to cope with big emotions.

After several months of being at home with Robbie and his older brother, the energy level in the house felt like a volcano about to erupt. We needed to leave the house and attempt to re-enter the normal world. The public school system was still offering only virtual schooling, but many small businesses were starting to open again. I needed to get both of my children out of the house just so they could move and burn off extra energy. Before the pandemic, Robbie had taken gymnastics classes, and he seemed to like them. Although he was with a group of other children, he was doing individual skills and could work at his own pace. The classes were helping him develop strength and coordination, and he came home feeling proud when he advanced to the next level. The gymnastics program had not reopened, but I did notice an advertisement for a local dance studio that offered a hip-hop dance class that included gymnastics. They called it Flip Hop, and the advertisement showed both boys and girls in the class.

I asked Robbie if he wanted to participate, and he immediately said yes. The next week, I took him to the dance studio. I didn't really have huge expectations for the class. I had previously taken Robbie to swim classes, beginner's soccer, and other activities, but except for gymnastics, he refused to go back after the first class. When the class ended, all the other children came out first, and when Robbie finally came out of the classroom, he was accompanied by the teacher. I thought she was going to tell me that he hid in the corner and didn't participate during the class. Instead, she asked me if this was Robbie's first dance class and if we had ever considered letting him take other types of dance lessons. She told me that Robbie was able to move to the beat and copy all the positions that she had demonstrated during class. Robbie asked if he could take other types of dance, so we signed him up for an additional evening of dance that included ballet and tap.

The studio had a video system that allowed me to watch Robbie's class and observe what he was doing. He was the youngest student in the flip-hop class, but he was modeling all of the teacher's movements. At home, Robbie is always moving his body, and in this class, that seemed to be an asset. He never stopped moving, but his body movements seemed controlled. When the teacher taught a new movement, all the students had time to practice it several times before the next skill was introduced. Robbie thrived on that type of repetition. Robbie never spoke during the class, but the teacher was right—his body was moving to the style and tempo of the music. Robbie was very flexible, so he loved all the complicated gymnastics moves that he got to do in class. He began asking to go to dance class every day, not just the days that he was signed up to attend.

As his class began to learn the routine for the spring recital, I saw Robbie repeatedly practice it at home. He had used his time in the evenings to move around and repeat those behaviors again and again, but now he was using the practice in a purposeful way. Even at seven years old, he was practicing daily without being asked—and he was so content when he was practicing. He started to practice certain complicated skills, such as an aerial (a cartwheel without his hands touching the ground). He was so devoted to the practice that he began to advance beyond the other children in his class simply due to his interest.

The preparation for the recital also required Robbie to interact with his classmates more than he typically would have preferred. Rehearsals did not require the children to speak to one another (which allowed Robbie to be on a more level playing field socially with the other children), but they still had to interact with one another by dancing simultaneously. This was probably the most amount of social interaction that Robbie could have handled at this point in his development, and it benefited him so much.

Pretty soon, the school staff began to notice the benefits that Robbie was experiencing from his dance classes. When Robbie was overwhelmed by big emotions at school, an assistant team would often take him out of the room to help him calm down and have some time to himself. After he became interested in dancing, the assistant teacher would take him out of the room, but Robbie would begin dancing to calm himself down without the assistant teacher prompting him. During recess, Robbie would use his free time to practice his dance skills, such as his aerial cartwheel. When other children saw him dance, they would come up to watch him and ask him about the skills he was demonstrating. His dancing became a conversation starter for him, and it helped him begin social interactions with his classmates. Even his music teacher began to make comments that Robbie's dance skills allowed him to experience music class in a different way, because he was always moving to the beat of the songs the class was listening to at the time.

Robbie has now been dancing for four years, and he is even a part of a competition dance team. Although he still struggles with direct attention from strangers (particularly engaging in conversation with people he does not know), Robbie can dance on stage in front of a large crowd. He does get nervous before he dances, but he has learned how to control his performance anxiety and still enjoy his dance piece. Robbie loves to do solo dances, but he enjoys the group performances as well. He still struggles with his facial expressions during performances and attempting to make eye contact with the audience, but he is improving. At home, he will choose a piece of music and create choreography to match the tone of the song. Even if he can't always express his emotions, he can dance to a piece of music that may match his emotions. Sometimes, I will ask him about the song he is dancing to when he is upset, and he will tell me that "he just feels dark." I am grateful for the way that dance has helped him to grow and overcome his challenges. When he was first diagnosed with autism, I was focused on finding him an occupational therapist and a child psychiatrist. I never thought about nontraditional treatments.

Our community has a magnet school for the creative and performing arts, and Robbie was accepted into the program as a dance major. Many of his school projects now allow him to use dance, music, or art as a way to reflect what he has learned. He has the opportunity to dance each day at school and uses that movement to help him regulate his emotions. Since it is a public magnet school, the school still follows his IEP, but I think allowing him to dance during school is already a huge way to individualize his education. Dance has given him the opportunity to express emotions and learn to be in social settings—things he would not have been able to accomplish without it. I know that dancing is not part of the curriculum for most education programs, but it has been my son's primary education tool and helped him progress in so many ways.

INTRODUCTION

I wrote this book because of my experiences as an educator and as a mother of a child who responds differently to the world in comparison to his peers and siblings. The goal is to provide information on learning tools that have worked for some children who are considered neurodivergent, so teachers can adapt their teaching techniques and help every student in their classrooms have an enjoyable learning experience. This book is meant to be a tool for early childhood and early elementary teachers, administrators, and parents of neurodivergent children.

Chapter 1 defines neurodivergence and describes the various conditions that are commonly considered part of neurodivergence (such as autism, ADHD, and dyslexia), highlighting the unique strengths and challenges that each can bring into the learning environment. Chapter 2 delves into understanding and accepting neurodivergent children and learning what is needed for a neurodiversity-affirming classroom.

Chapters 3 and 4 discuss the classroom environment and describe how to create a sensory-friendly classroom and how to use your classroom aesthetics to construct a learning environment that benefits all children. These two chapters are followed by chapter 5 on the outdoor classroom.

Chapters 6, 7, 8, and 9 look at the applications of dance and movement, mindfulness, art, music, and animal-assisted therapies in the classroom and how they benefit both neurodivergent and neurotypical children.

Finally, chapters 10, 11, and 12 explore how to foster self-advocacy in young learners, engage families effectively, and assess children's progress thoughtfully and affirmatively.

CHAPTER 1:

Defining Neurodivergence

We have long understood that each snowflake is unique. Slight variations in their form and structure make them each different from one another. Variables such as the temperature and humidity of the environment affect their size and composition. Snowflakes are all formed by the crystallization of water, but that still allows for an infinite number of different patterns, and some of those differences may only be detectable under a microscope.

Along those same lines, with over eight billion people in the world, it is understood that each of those individuals is different from one another (Institut National D'Etudes Demographiques [INED], 2024). Genetically, they have different physical traits, from eye color to height. It is also important to remember that the environmental factors that each individual has experienced contribute to that person's temperament and health. The location in which the person lives shapes their cultural influences, the language they speak, and the other people with whom they have interacted during a lifetime. Environmental experiences have a huge effect, particularly if a child is exposed to adverse childhood experiences compared to positive experiences during their most influential years (Cabrera et al., 2022). These environmental experiences could lead identical twins in completely different directions socially and emotionally.

Despite the understanding that nature and nurture both contribute to creating individuals with unique traits, for many years, researchers believed that the body systems—especially the brain—had the same operating system within each person (Maryville University, 2020). There was an assumption that all functioning human beings had brains that took in information and processed it the same way. The original treatment plans for autism were to make autistic individuals function like normal individuals. The autism researcher Laurent Mottron challenged the scientific community not to change these neurodiverse individuals but to support them in a way that allows them to still be themselves (Harvard Health, 2017). Researchers previously believed that if the individual's brain did not operate in the normal pattern, then there was something "broken" with that person. Only in the past few decades have specialists begun to identify people who are productive members of society yet seem to have a completely different manner of relating to the world.

These individuals have always existed. For example, Albert Einstein was a mathematical and scientific genius. His research contributions allowed the world to understand complicated subjects such as the theory of relativity, how space and time relate to an individual's own motion and place in the universe. Despite his intense knowledge of science, his development in early childhood did not follow the typical path followed by most of his peers (PBS, 1998). He did not learn to speak at the same age as his peers, and he did not do well in a traditional school setting. His parents became worried and sought out the advice of a doctor because he did not fit the typical mold of a successful child. Yet, his accomplishments went on to outshine anyone of the time. The issue was that he did not meet the typical expectations for learning.

With more research on human development and brain research, it has become obvious that most people develop in the same pattern, and their brains ingest and process information in the same manner. It is also obvious that some individuals do not respond to the world in the same way as others, but at the same time, they are not damaged, just different. The brain is still functioning and operating as the chief administration system of the body, but the operating system is different. Let's begin by understanding what it means to be *neurodivergent*.

Establishing a Definition for Neurodivergence

If the brain is compared to a computer, most human beings would be operating on the same software, and information easily transfers from one computer to another since it is processed in the same way. However, a small group of computers is using a different software system. Those computers are still productive and processing information. The difficulty may arise when one software system tries to communicate with another software system.

Communication is possible, but it may take more time to decode the information. Both software systems work, but since most computers use the same software, some may feel that everyone should switch to the majority system. Unfortunately, since this involves the brain instead of a computer system, it isn't possible to switch software. We are going to have to learn how to operate and appreciate each other's differences. The individuals in the majority would be considered *neurotypical* because their brains are operating in a manner that is expected. Those in the minority would be considered *neurodivergent*. They are different from the majority, but those differences are neither right nor wrong.

The word *neurodivergent* has become much more common in casual conversation, but it still carries a fair amount of mystery around it. Most people associate it with autism, but autism is only one diagnosis that falls into the neurodivergent category. Although autism numbers appear to be growing, far more individuals are neurodivergent than those who simply have an autism diagnosis (Centers for Disease Control and Prevention [CDC], 2023). Others may see the word as a trendy way to express their personality differences. Still another group may think that the term *neurodivergent* allows a small sect of individuals to receive preferential treatment when there are no visible differences that separate those who are neurodivergent and neurotypical (Pryal, 2024).

The true definition of *neurodivergent* has several key components:

- *Neurodivergent* is a nonmedical term that describes individuals whose brains work differently from the majority (Cleveland Clinic, 2025e).
- Neurodivergence can be associated with a medical diagnosis, but it does not have to be.
- One of the foundations of the neurodiversity movement is that these variations creating neurodivergence are natural and a valuable part of the individual (Kapp, 2020). Neurodivergence does not need to be fixed or cured. (However, medical complications from a diagnosis that exists along with neurodivergence may still need treatment.)

What Conditions Are Included in Neurodivergence?

Many organizations such as the American Academy of Pediatrics (AAP), the American Psychological Association (APA), the Cleveland Clinic, and others have established lists of what types of diagnoses fall into the category of neurodivergence (Broder-Fingert and Abate, 2022; APA Member Services, 2023; Cleveland Clinic, 2025e). Although some lists may be more extensive than others, most organizations and hospitals agree on a succinct list of conditions that are considered neurodivergent.

Autism Spectrum Disorder

Autism spectrum disorder is a developmental disorder that affects the neurological system as well as the individual's social and emotional development (National Institute of Mental Health, 2025a). It is called a spectrum disorder because it can present differently in each individual with the condition. Some of the most common characteristics of autism spectrum disorder include:

- Difficulty with verbal and nonverbal communication with others
- Repetitive behaviors (stim behavior) and deep interests
- Difficulty adjusting to new environments or changes in routine
- Difficulty processing strong emotions or identifying the emotions of others
- Easily overwhelmed by intense sensory experiences such as loud noises, textures, and smells
- Difficulty with sleep patterns (National Autistic Society, 2020)

An individual with autism spectrum disorder may not have all of these characteristics. Some individuals have extensive verbal skills, while others may be nonverbal. Some people with the diagnosis may have a cognitive delay, but others may not. Some children and adults with autism make eye contact while talking, while others may struggle to do so. The spectrum disorder does not progress from good to bad. Instead, it is more like a pie graph in which each characteristic is individualized for the person with the diagnosis. Think of a pie graph with sections that include items such as social communication, stim behaviors (see page 17 for more information), routines, obsessions (or deep interests), sensory dysfunction, executive dysfunction, regulating emotions (meltdowns), and aggression. Some people may be able to process sensory stimulation but not regulate their emotions without meltdowns.

These same individuals may have significant strengths due to their diagnosis. Many individuals with autism spectrum disorder may have a great memory for details and remember pictures and patterns. Others may be strong students and stand out in subjects such as math, science, and the arts, where many neurotypical learners struggle. Many students with autism spectrum disorder can learn through sound and pictures, so they can excel in school even if they are nontraditional learners. Remember that each neurodivergent condition has its strengths as well as challenges.

Treatment for autism spectrum disorder can vary based on the characteristics that the individual shows. Many doctors will recommend pediatric therapy, particularly speech and occupational therapy, to help children and adults learn to develop social relationships and communicate with others. Depending on secondary conditions, such as social anxiety or problems sleeping, then doctors may also recommend medication. Most children with autism spectrum disorder will need special education to make sure that social and emotional delays do not affect academic growth.

Attention Deficit Hyperactivity Disorder

Attention deficit hyperactivity disorder (ADHD) is a neurological or mental health disorder that can cause a lack of focus, hyperactivity, impulsive actions, and even aggression (American Psychiatric Association, 2025). It is a relatively common diagnosis in children, but there is some speculation that it may be overdiagnosed, particularly in boys (Kazda et al., 2021). The diagnosis should not be issued prior to beginning elementary school because the characteristics of impulsivity, lack of focus, and hyperactivity are developmentally appropriate in the preschool age range. Once a child enters elementary school, the condition may affect their ability to function in the classroom, complete daily life tasks, and have productive social relationships.

There are three types of ADHD:

- Primarily focused on inattention
- Primarily focused on hyperactivity
- A combination of inattention and hyperactivity (CDC, 2024)

To diagnose ADHD, the child psychologist will make sure that the symptoms have been present for at least six months and that the child demonstrates the symptoms in more than one setting. For example, if the symptoms are only present in the classroom, then the organization of the space could be contributing to the child's lack of focus, disorganization, and hyperactivity. However, if the symptoms are present at both home and school, it is more likely that the child does have ADHD.

A child who has hyperactive ADHD often will:

- not remain in their seat during class time,
- be moving and fidgeting,
- talk constantly,
- have difficulty waiting for their turn,
- run through the classroom or home when it isn't safe or necessary,
- be unable to play quietly, and
- interrupt others.

A child who has inattentive ADHD often will:

- stare off into space,
- not complete tasks,
- lose items frequently,
- forget essential daily activities,
- not listen when spoken to,
- not follow instructions, and
- become mentally overwhelmed attempting to complete simple tasks because of the focus required.

If a child has a combination of the two types of ADHD, then symptoms from both lists can be present.

Treatment for ADHD typically involves a combination of cognitive therapy (talk therapy) and medication. Some specialists will recommend that families and children go to therapy together to establish better rules and routines in the home. A child does not need special education simply because of an ADHD diagnosis. Instead, the school may encourage a 504 Plan, which is established through the Vocational Rehabilitation Act of 1973 (Anzilotti, 2023). Instead of working with special educators, the 504 Plan simply guarantees the child accommodations needed to be successful, such as additional time to take a test or the ability to take movement breaks throughout the day after sitting still too long (California State Council on Developmental Disabilities, n.d.).

Tourette's Syndrome

Tourette's syndrome is a neurological disorder in which the person has uncontrolled repetitive movements or uncontrolled sounds (called *tics*) (Mayo Clinic, 2025e). The condition typically emerges around six years of age, and 75 percent of the cases are found in boys and men. The condition can be mild, or it can range in severity to the point that it constantly disrupts daily life. The tics (movement or sound) can be brief and cause little disruption, or they can be considered complex and disrupt multiple muscle groups in a coordinated pattern.

Simple tics can include:

- Shoulder shrugging
- Eye blinking
- Throat clearing
- Grunting

- Nose twitching
- Uncontrolled mouth movement
- Head jerking
- Eyes quickly moving back and forth
- Coughing
- Barking

Complex tics can include:

- Repeated visible movements
- Patterned leg or arm movements
- Jumping or hopping
- Smelling objects
- Rude gestures
- Repeating others' words and phrases
- Using rude language

Tics will increase with stress, lack of sleep, or illness, when the body's defenses are lower. They can also occur when the person is sleeping. Many individuals with Tourette's syndrome will experience an increase in tics during puberty. Most people experiencing tics will know in advance that a tic is coming. If the tic is mild, the individual may be able to stop its occurrence. More moderate or severe tics make the person's body uncomfortable as they approach, and the only relief is for the tic to occur. Also, it is possible to have tics without having Tourette's syndrome. The tics are a neurological symptom and could indicate a different neurological condition. However, Tourette's syndrome is based on a diagnosis of simple and complex tics occurring consistently over time. Many people with the condition eventually learn to control the tics, but they are usually uncontrolled during childhood and the teen years.

Obsessive-Compulsive Disorder

Obsessive-compulsive disorder is a mental health diagnosis where individuals experience frequent and uncontrolled thoughts accompanied by consistent repetitive behaviors (obsessions and compulsions) (National Institute of Mental Health, 2025c). The obsessive thoughts are unwanted and continuously increase the person's anxiety. The obsession could focus on fear of germs, fear of losing something, fear of being unable to control your behavior, focus on wanting everything symmetrical, aggressive thoughts, or inappropriate thoughts. Once the person has the obsessive thoughts, then they do the compulsive behavior as a response. For example, someone obsessed with thinking about germs and illness may begin obsessively cleaning in response. Other compulsions may include organizing, double-checking if doors are locked, counting, praying, or repeating familiar rhymes or mantras.

Many people want to have a clean or organized home. Other individuals are careful to lock their door when they are home alone. This does not mean that they have obsessive-compulsive disorder. To be diagnosed with the disorder, the behaviors would need to disrupt the individual's life significantly. Some indications may be:

- having no control over the obsessions and compulsions, even if the individual can identify that they have gone too far.
- spending more than one hour per day focused on obsessions and compulsions.
- disrupting daily life activities to perform obsessions and compulsions.
- experiencing stress from the obsessions and experiencing a small amount of relief from the compulsions.

Although obsessive-compulsive disorder typically starts in late childhood to young adulthood, it can affect younger children. If it does affect a child, it is most likely that the child will not understand what is happening, and a parent or teacher will more likely identify the concern. Obsessive-compulsive disorder can progress over time to be more debilitating, but it can also be managed. Like many other mental health diagnoses, obsessive-compulsive disorder can be managed with a combination of therapy and medication.

Bipolar Disorder

Bipolar disorder is a mental health condition that causes dramatic shifts in a person's mood and activity level (National Institute of Mental Health, 2025b). This illness was previously called manic-depressive disorder because those with the diagnosis would experience periods of mania (high energy, lack of concentration, and stress), then switch to periods of depression with low energy levels and sad or hopeless periods. Although this condition will typically present during adolescence or later, some children experience bipolar disorder. During a "cycle" of the illness, the patient will experience the manic episode first, followed by the depressive stage.

Epilepsy

Epilepsy is a neurological condition that causes the body to have recurring seizures (Mayo Clinic, 2025c). With epilepsy, the electrical surges that typically operate throughout the brain to carry messages seem to malfunction, and the result of that malfunction is a seizure. Having one seizure does not mean that someone has epilepsy; a seizure can occur with a high fever, head injury, or other trigger. Doctors typically look to see if someone has had two unexplained seizures within a small time period before offering a diagnosis of epilepsy. There is no one specific cause of epilepsy; it can be attributed to genetics, head trauma, an infection in the brain, or secondary illnesses. Some people may be diagnosed with idiopathic epilepsy, which means there is no detectable reason that the person is having seizures.

A seizure may only involve one part of the brain. This would be called a *focal seizure*. *Generalized seizures* include the whole brain. Some of the most common displays of seizures include *absence seizures,* in which the individual appears to stare off into space and show no response to the world around them, and *tonic-clonic seizures*, which is the most dramatic type of seizure and involves a loss of consciousness followed by the individual falling to the ground and having large muscle convulsions. It is obvious when someone has a tonic-clonic seizure, but absence seizures could go undetected for quite a while.

Individuals with epilepsy typically treat the condition with a variety of different medications; however, it is also important to be aware of common triggers that could make the individual more likely to have a seizure. Some of these triggers include lack of sleep, stress, flashing lights (strobes), hormone changes, alcohol use, skipping a dose of seizure medication, illness, dehydration, or illicit drug use.

Although epilepsy is a diagnosis that affects the brain, it does not mean that someone with epilepsy is not smart. Many individuals with epilepsy are highly intelligent, despite having seizures. It is also important to remember that epilepsy is not a diagnosis that focuses on one type of person. Anyone can have a seizure, although there are some medical diagnoses, such as ADHD or depression, that may make it more likely to also have seizures (Sirven and Shafer, 2014).

Prader-Willi Syndrome

Prader-Willi syndrome is a genetic condition that affects the physical development, mental health, and behavioral systems of the body (Mayo Clinic, 2025d). The key indicator of Prader-Willi syndrome is that the individual always feels hungry. Individuals with Prader-Willi syndrome want to eat because they never feel full, which can lead to obesity and health complications caused by obesity.

Prader-Willi syndrome can arise in infancy. Some of the most common symptoms include:

- poor muscle tone;
- poor sucking reflex;
- distinct facial features such as almond-shaped eyes, thin upper lip, narrowing of the head starting at the temples, and a down-turned mouth;
- poor responsiveness to stimuli; and
- difficulty waking up and low energy level (Mayo Clinic, 2025d).

As individuals with Prader-Willi syndrome grow into childhood, they will be driven by an urge to eat, and they will begin to gain excess weight. Their bodies do not typically make enough growth hormone, so they will display poor physical growth. The diagnosis also includes cognitive impairment and poor motor skills. Individuals with Prader-Willi syndrome will typically have behavioral issues such as emotional meltdowns, anger outbursts, and manipulative behaviors. Many of these behaviors will be a result of the child trying to obtain more food.

Prader-Willi syndrome is usually accompanied by obesity-related symptoms and complications. Those complications can include:

- Type 2 diabetes
- High blood pressure
- High cholesterol
- Sleep apnea
- Heart disease

Due to all the health implications of the diagnosis, it is wise for the family to work closely with a doctor and therapeutic specialists to create the best plan for growth and development.

Social Anxiety

Social anxiety is a mental health diagnosis that causes children and adults to constantly be anxious about being watched or judged by others (National Institute of Mental Health, n.d.). Although some people may think of social anxiety as shyness, this level of anxiety typically limits the person's ability to live a normal life without support and treatment. A true diagnosis of social anxiety means that the individual's fear and anxiety are interfering with school, work, and normal daily living. Someone with social anxiety may stay awake all night worrying about a social interaction that could occur the next day. Sometimes, these fears are rational, but at times the fears are irrational yet still consume the individual's time.

When an individual is experiencing bouts of social anxiety, typical symptoms may include:

- Sweating or shaking
- Extreme blushing
- Experiencing a "fight or flight" reaction
- Forgetting what to say
- Having an upset stomach
- Losing control of voice volume or having a dry mouth
- Inability to make eye contact
- Avoiding certain situations altogether

Treatment for social anxiety may include cognitive behavioral therapy (talk therapy) and medication. Medication has been an effective tool to assist with anxiety, but sometimes those medications may have side effects that also make the individual anxious. A doctor would have to select the medication that best meets the needs of the patient. Anxiety does not have a symptom of cognitive impairment, and in many cases, anxiety may be worse for those with higher cognitive skills than for individuals who are typically developing. Highly intelligent children may be more prone to anxiety because they can worry about a wide variety of events that could occur, even if they are unlikely (Post, 2022).

Irlen Syndrome

Irlen syndrome is a type of visual dyslexia that affects how the brain identifies light sources and colors (Irlen Diagnostic Clinics, 2025). Individuals with Irlen syndrome may also have handwriting difficulties, auditory difficulties, eye-muscle spasms, hyperactivity, allergies, and feelings of being "stupid" or "inadequate." The person typically experiences optical distortions that make it difficult to process visual stimuli, which leads to complications with finishing work and getting answers correct. These students are intelligent, but they have difficulty processing information in the manner expected, so they could be labeled as lazy. People with Irlen syndrome can also experience physical symptoms such as headaches and nausea, which are common with other disorders when the optic nerve is affected. It is important to remember that there is no problem with the optic nerve itself but with how the brain interprets the information collected by the optic nerve.

The most common treatment for Irlen syndrome is a prescription for special glasses that control the amount of light the individual takes in at one time. Glasses with colored lenses tailored to the individual's needs can control the wavelength of light and reduce interference as the brain processes information from the optic nerve. The prescription may need to be adjusted over time and as a child grows.

Dyscalculia

Dyscalculia is a learning disability that affects the brain's ability to understand and interpret numbers and symbols (Cleveland Clinic, 2025a). This does not mean that the individual is not intelligent. Instead, the brain seems to be confused by mathematical symbols, so it is more challenging for these individuals to learn math concepts. The symptoms of dyscalculia emerge in childhood when children first begin learning the concepts of math, but many adults may go through their whole lives without knowing they have dyscalculia. These adults often think they are just bad at mathematics, but instead, there is a developmental reason they are struggling.

Dyscalculia affects visual processing, short-term and long-term memory, the understanding of quantity, and the understanding of calculation. It also makes it difficult to communicate a concept to someone else. Individuals with dyscalculia will often develop anxiety over doing mathematics and become highly agitated during the process of mathematical computation. The stress of completing mathematical problems may cause physical symptoms such as nausea or sweating.

Teachers are usually the first to notice the signs of dyscalculia in children, although there is no specific test that diagnoses the condition. It is best to begin treatment for dyscalculia as early as possible, since the brain of a young child has not finished developing and can be trained. Special educators can work with children with dyscalculia to help them better decode numbers and calculations.

Dysgraphia

Dysgraphia is a condition where the individual has a difficult time turning thoughts into written words (Cleveland Clinic, 2025b). This is sometimes classified as a written language learning disability. Again, a learning disability does not indicate that the child or adult is not intelligent. Instead, the brain is having difficulty processing the information in the manner expected, so it must learn how to decode the information in a new manner. Dysgraphia affects fine motor skills, spatial recognition, memory skills, language processing, organization, and conceptualization. Children who have dysgraphia may:

- Have difficulty holding a crayon or pencil
- Have difficulty writing in a straight line
- Write letters in reverse
- Have difficulty remembering how to write a letter
- Have a hard time creating and writing a sentence
- Omit important words from sentences
- Place words in the wrong order in a sentence

Similar to dyscalculia, a teacher is most likely to be the first person to detect this condition. Most preschool students are not developmentally ready for writing skills, so this delay would not emerge until elementary school. Once a specialist confirms that the child has dysgraphia, then it would be essential to implement special education training to help the child overcome the decoding difficulties.

Dyslexia

Dyslexia is one of the more well-known disabilities. It is a condition that causes reading to be difficult because of complications with decoding letters and words, along with identifying speech sounds (Mayo Clinic, 2025b). Dyslexia does not affect the child's cognitive function, and in many cases, the child can be intelligent but simply struggle with the decoding process. The good news is that many children diagnosed with dyslexia can go on to be successful in school. The sooner the condition is identified, then the sooner the interventions can begin to help and allow the child to overcome the decoding challenges. There is often an emotional component to dyslexia in which children feel inadequate and unsuccessful with their school work. It essential for a mentor or educator to encourage the child to understand that dyslexia is not linked to intelligence. Once again, the brain simply processes information differently and needs a little bit of guidance.

Although dyslexia should not be diagnosed in preschool or early childhood education programs, some symptoms may begin to show before a child is in a structured elementary school environment. Those traits include:

- Delayed speech development and difficulty mastering new vocabulary
- Difficulty learning new sound patterns for words or consistently pronouncing words incorrectly
- Struggling with songs and stories that require a child to repeat rhyming patterns
- Difficulty learning the names of letters, numbers, or colors

Dyslexia does not mean that a child simply prints letters backwards when first learning to write. That is developmentally appropriate when children are first learning to write and form letters. Instead, the characteristics of dyslexia are much more pervasive when children are in elementary school. The traits that may show a child needs to be evaluated for dyslexia include:

- Reading skills that are obviously below the child's grade level
- Difficulty processing information that is heard
- Persistent spelling challenges
- Trouble answering questions and finding the right word to express oneself

- Sequencing difficulties (letters in a word, events in a chain of events)
- Taking a long time to read passages of information or avoiding reading if at all possible
- Difficulty sounding out words

A child with dyslexia can qualify for an IEP and receive reading supports during the school day. Families can also access reading support programs in the community to support children with reading challenges such as dyslexia.

Dyspraxia

Dyspraxia affects a child's physical movement and coordination (Cleveland Clinic, 2025c). Both the large muscle movements and the small muscle movements are affected with dyspraxia, particularly since strong gross motor (large muscle) skills are necessary to be able to develop strong fine motor (hand muscle) skills. A child with dyspraxia has working muscles (different from apraxia where muscles may degenerate over time), but they lack refined muscle movement. Dyspraxia is more likely to affect children who have been born prematurely (prior to thirty-seven weeks of pregnancy), and it is more likely to affect males than females. Only about 6 percent of children in elementary school will show signs of dyspraxia.

The biggest indicator of dyspraxia in infants and toddlers is that the children are not meeting their developmental milestones for physical development. This would involve many of the skills that families look forward to seeing, such as when a child rolls over, sits up, crawls, stands up, and walks. Some of the more complicated skills that a child with dyspraxia may struggle with include playing with toys (shape sorter, ring stacker, etc.) and being able to use a spoon and fork. As children with dyspraxia approach preschool, they may have difficulty with:

- Walking up and down stairs, particularly with alternating feet on steps
- Balance, such as seeming to needlessly move his body frequently, which could lead to falling into things and bumping into surfaces
- Coordination, such as catching and throwing or riding a scooter or bike
- Basic sports such as kicking a ball in soccer or catching in baseball
- Independence skills such as feeding oneself, brushing teeth, and getting dressed independently
- Writing, using scissors, and other activities that require a lot of fine motor coordination

These children may be thought of as lazy or lethargic, but motor skills are simply difficult and discouraging for many children with dyspraxia. If these children don't seem willing to participate in energetic and athletic activities, then that could cause them to have weight problems due to inactivity.

In most cases, a child with dyspraxia may work with a team of specialists that includes an occupational or physical therapist and a neurologist. Since this condition occurs because of the way the brain processes movement, the neurologist can be an essential part of the treatment team. Most children with dyspraxia work on task-oriented treatment, learning and practicing specific skills needed at school and in daily life. Since motor skills can greatly affect academic learning, such as the ability to write, then dyspraxia can be addressed in a special education plan. Many families may seek additional therapy outside of school to work on improving many basic living skills and recreation skills.

Strengths in Neurodiversity

Although many neurodivergent conditions come with a medical diagnosis that has some negative side effects, the neurodivergent condition itself is not a negative thing. Individuals who are neurodivergent show that their cognitive processing is slightly different from the norm of society as a whole, also show many strengths. It is important that these strengths are recognized and even celebrated. It is quite probable that if neurodivergent children and adults did not process information in a slightly different manner, then these positive strengths would not present themselves either.

Analytical and Logical Thinking

First, research has shown that many individuals with neurodivergent conditions show a strong aptitude for analytical and logical thinking (Austin and Pisano, 2017). This can include a strong memory, and in some cases, an eidetic memory (which is what the public often thinks of as a "photographic" memory, when individuals remember based on pictures, sounds, and other sensory information). The same individuals may have an aptitude for math and technology. It is common for these individuals to have strong attention to detail and the ability to recognize patterns or identify problems with which neurotypical individuals may struggle at times.

One obvious reason that neurodivergence is a strength is that the brain works differently, so a neurodivergent individual has the opportunity to look at a situation differently from everyone else. This leads to innovation and creativity that doing things "the same old way" just won't allow (Palumbo, 2024). By looking at the situation in a different light, creative solutions naturally evolve.

Deep Interests

Another strength of someone who is neurodivergent is their tendency to have deep interests (Ashinoff and Abu-Akel, 2019). Many neurodivergent individuals develop interests in a topic that causes them to ask more questions and learn more about that topic than anyone else. At one point, the disability community may have called this an obsession; however, these deep interests do not typically harm anyone and usually lead to greater knowledge. With that viewpoint, the disability community has moved away from the negative connotation associated with *obsession* and has started to look at the wealth of knowledge that is highlighted with these deep interests. The media may depict neurodivergent children to be obsessed with trains or large construction equipment; however, we also see neurodivergent adults such as Albert Einstein or Temple Grandin whose deep interests have led to remarkable discoveries in science. These deep interests can allow a child to become gifted in the arts, sports, or academic areas simply due to the amount of time that they spend learning about that field.

Strong Sense of Right and Wrong

Although many children and adults with a neurodivergent condition may have some type of social or emotional delay, they may also have some social and emotional skills that are advanced. Many neurodivergent individuals have a strong sense of right and wrong (Coupé, 2023). That component of their personality motivates them to have a great deal of loyalty and a strong sense of social justice. It may also motivate them to be consistently honest, even when it is difficult. A hyperfocus and deep interest in certain topics allows for individuals to be persistent and determined.

Howard Gardner is famous for his theory of multiple intelligences, which go far beyond simply acknowledging academic skills as a way to measure intelligence (Vromen, 2023). With a similar type of lens, it is possible to view the different strengths that are present with neurodiversity. Academic intelligence is one of the strengths, but also, the creative and innovative viewpoint is key when analyzing how a neurodivergent individual views the world.

Challenges Associated with Neurodiversity

Along with strengths, neurodivergent children and adults also face challenges each day. In most cases, therapeutic measures can help them be successful despite these challenges. After reviewing many of the disabilities and medical conditions that fall into the neurodivergent classification, it is easy to see that some of the conditions are specific and have characteristics that only apply to that particular medical diagnosis. However, other challenges apply to most of the individuals considered to be neurodivergent. Since each child and adult is different, they may not exhibit all of these traits, or some traits may be much stronger than others. Each person will be different, but certain characteristics are frequently present in most neurodivergent people.

Stimming

The term *stimming* stands for self-stimulation (Velkoff, 2025). Stimming is typically when a person performs repetitive body movements to help regulate the body. Stimming can also be used to express emotions or for enjoyment. Some of the most common stim behaviors for neurodivergent children include:

- Rocking back and forth
- Twirling hair
- Biting fingernails
- Flapping hands
- Chewing or lip smacking
- Spinning or twirling
- Visual stimming/intensely staring
- Finger flicking
- Head banging (or self-injurious behaviors)

Stim behaviors typically increase when a child is under high amounts of stress. Although these behaviors may draw attention from others because they don't seem typical, they do not need to be stopped unless they are harmful to the child or others. If the child is using the stim behaviors to calm down independently, then they are helping the child to be autonomous.

Masking

For neurodivergent individuals, masking is a way to hide their true selves and attempt to show "normal" behaviors (Cleveland Clinic, 2024). Masking helps the child to display social norms in settings when the child feels that normal behavior would be more acceptable. In some ways, all individuals mask their behaviors when they are in settings where they feel they need to act differently to be socially acceptable. Unfortunately, neurodivergent children may exhibit masking frequently to feel they fit into the classroom or social setting.

When children are masking their typical behavior, it means that they feel their typical behaviors are wrong or inappropriate. Continued masking is not healthy for a child because it means that the children are dwelling on what parts of their behaviors are "wrong" and having consistent negative thoughts. Masking can also be exhausting. Attempting to demonstrate a behavior that is difficult for a child, such as maintaining eye contact all day, can cause a child to be physically and mentally exhausted. Neurodivergent children ultimately need an environment where they are allowed to exhibit their natural behaviors, such as stimming, as long as the behaviors are not going to injure the child or others. Children who are in situations where they feel the need to mask their behaviors consistently are at greater risk of developing anxiety or depression (Cleveland Clinic, 2024).

Dysregulation

Emotional dysregulation is a term used when a child's emotions are out of control and the child does not feel that they can control their feelings (Cleveland Clinic, 2025d). Since neurodivergent individuals' brains operate slightly differently from others', their emotions also operate differently. When it is hard for a child or adult to identify their emotions, it can also be hard to process and control their emotions. Emotional regulation is a skill that is typically learned in childhood; however, many neurodivergent children have a developmental delay with their social and emotional skills. When other children are learning to control their emotions, neurodivergent children may still be trying to understand the emotions they feel or attempting to identify the emotions of others. Sometimes, their emotions are so big that the child cannot process the emotion, and the child is completely overwhelmed. Although it may appear that the child is having a temper tantrum due to the outpouring of emotion, this is not the case. A temper tantrum is actually an emotional tool that a child uses to manipulate a situation. During emotional outbursts from a neurodivergent child, the child has no control over their emotions and cannot be rational until the emotions resolve.

When observing a child who experiences emotional dysregulation, they may demonstrate:

- Mood swings
- Mania, for example, easily excitable, agitated, or extremely energetic
- Impulsive behavior
- Irritability
- Depression
- Being prone to emotional outbursts
- Disproportionate responses to frustration

Because of the severity of emotional dysregulation, the mood swings and emotional outbursts may dominate the child's life. This lack of emotional control could prevent the child from forming friendships, participating in group settings, and having a normal family life. The emotional uncertainty could also place a great deal of stress on the family members living with the child.

Communication Skills

Communication skills affect neurodivergent children in a number of ways (Mayo Clinic, 2025a). Some children with a neurodivergent condition may be nonverbal or have a speech impairment that prevents them from being able to communicate with others. This does not mean that these children have nothing to say. Many children with speech impairments still have a high level of cognitive function, but they may struggle because weak muscles prevent them from articulating words. Other children may have difficulty with finding a way to organize their thoughts so others will understand them.

Other neurodivergent children have the ability to speak but may have challenges with communication skills. For example, these children may struggle to make eye contact, lack facial expression, or have a hard time finding the appropriate amount of physical space needed when having a conversation with another person. Other symptoms may include:

- Playing alone instead of with same-age peers
- Not responding when they hear their names called
- Not preferring to be held or touched
- Speaking with an odd pattern to their speech or at an unusually loud volume
- Having difficulty entering a conversation with peers and possibly approaching a conversation with aggression or with too much enthusiasm
- Having a difficult time reading the facial expressions or nonverbal cues of others

Although many neurodivergent children prefer to spend time alone, these children should receive support learning how to be in social situations successfully with others. Both speech pathologists and occupational therapists can support children who need assistance with communication skills. If the child experiences social anxiety that contributes to communication deficits, then a mental health specialist may also be able to assist the child in increasing these skills.

Sensory Processing Dysfunction

Many neurodivergent children struggle with how they process sensory information (Krauss, 2024). A great deal of information comes to the brain through sight, sound, smell, taste, and touch. Additionally, the brain receives information from the proprioceptive sense, interoceptive sense, and the vestibular sense. The *proprioceptive sense* is responsible for detecting the body's posture and position, as well as how the bones, joints, and muscles work together (ScienceDirect, 2024). The *interoceptive sense* is aware of the body sensations such as hunger, feeling tired, and feeling muscle tension. The *vestibular sense* is how the body feels as it moves through space. It is based in the inner ear and coordinates with balance, vision, and the proprioceptive sense. These will be discussed further in chapter 3.

In many cases, a neurodivergent child will either be easily overwhelmed by sensory information or will crave more sensory information and will exhibit behaviors that allow the child to experience more sensory information. For example, a child who is overwhelmed by too much sensory information, may:

- react aggressively to a classroom with clutter and objects hanging from the ceiling.
- hide or cover their ears when all the students are talking at once or loud music is playing.
- run away from strong smells.
- throw or refuse to eat food that is spicy or too salty.

A child who is seeking more sensory input may:

- jump off of furniture or playground equipment to feel the pressure on muscles and joints when they land.
- charge into groups and knock down peers to experience physical contact.
- scream or speak at a large volume just to hear more noise.
- request and eat foods and condiments with strong flavors such as hot sauce, pepper, lemons, or salsa.
- spin around in circles to feel their center of gravity.

To help children with sensory dysfunction be as successful as possible in the classroom setting, provide them with a variety of appropriate sensory experiences as part of the learning process, and help them understand which behaviors are safe and which are not. It is also key for teachers and parents to understand that sensory experiences that are tolerable or pleasant for some children can be overwhelming for others. The classroom and home environments have to allow children to explore with their senses without providing so much sensory information that the brain cannot handle it.

Challenging Behaviors

Unfortunately, when communication and emotional-regulation skills are placed under stress, neurodivergent children can resort to aggressive behavior as a way of protecting themselves (Purba, Febriyana, and Setiawati, 2024). The most common aggressive behaviors seen in neurodivergent children include intense emotional outbursts, self-injurious behaviors, or attempting to hit, kick, or bite others. These behaviors typically arise when the child is angry, frustrated, or anxious. They can also result from strong emotions that the child does not know how to express or from being overwhelmed by sensory input. Some children will become anxious when their consistent routines are changed without warning or when they are introduced to new people or situations for which expectations have not been established. When a neurodivergent child becomes overly anxious, they can react in a fight-or-flight pattern. The aggressive behaviors come out when the child believes that they need to fight to be safe.

Some researchers believe that these extreme aggressive behaviors occur when a child is in a classroom or a home life that is overly harsh and doesn't allow for the child's natural differences (Purba, Febriyana, and Setiawati, 2024). Some research also shows that hormones and chemical imbalances in the brain, such as levels of serotonin, contribute to aggression (Siever, 2008). Many doctors will recommend medication once aggressive behaviors emerge, but doctors and families should consider whether the child's natural environment allows for neurodivergent differences. For example, if a child is disciplined for stim behaviors that help with natural self-regulation, then aggression can build up when the child lacks a method for self-calming. A child can also become angry and frustrated when the learning environment is only designed for typical learning (for example, with children sitting in seats and listening to the teacher for extended periods of time). To be successful, nontraditional learners will need outlets such as movement breaks, breaks from social interactions, and the right sensory balance.

Despite the challenges associated with neurodivergent conditions, each child has an opportunity to enjoy school and to enjoy learning. The key is to take a strengths-based approach and help children overcome their challenges. Overall, the key to nurturing a neurodivergent child includes finding the learning tools that work for that child and the teacher's willingness to try new techniques. By using more creative approaches, such as creative arts or the outdoor classroom, children may be able to flourish in a less traditional classroom setting. The following chapters will offer teachers and families ideas to help neurodivergent children use different approaches to learn the required classroom content.

CHAPTER 2:

Understanding and Acceptance

Although many neurodivergent individuals live full and productive lives, one of the greatest challenges of neurodiversity can be the misconceptions and myths held by others in the community or within the families of neurodivergent children and adults. Parents and caregivers can typically be a child's fiercest advocates, yet other family members may hold divisive views on neurodiversity. Those in the community who don't know a neurodivergent individual personally may hold onto beliefs they have been exposed to in the media. These uneducated perspectives can lead to hurt feelings and defensive reactions, particularly when they are used in direct conversations. In the following list, I have included some of the most common and painful statements. Each of these statements is based on a lack of information, and it is important to share factual information to combat these myths. Following each statement is a summary of some key facts that can help educate the general population about neurodiversity.

- "You don't look neurodivergent to me." Although many disabilities and medical diagnoses may be associated with certain physical traits, a large number of conditions are categorized as "invisible disabilities." Invisible disabilities are not detectable by simply looking at an individual, but they can still have a profound effect on the person's daily living (National Institutes of Health, 2024). Just as it is inappropriate to judge someone's quality of life by visibly assessing their race or gender, it is also inappropriate to estimate whether or not a person has a disability by simply looking at them.

- "Everyone is a little neurodivergent, right?" Neurodiversity is composed of and diagnosed by a long list of both positive and negative traits. As with any diagnosable condition, it would be easy to go through that list and find a few characteristics that apply to yourself. Many individuals experience anxiety. Many individuals are overwhelmed by the sensory input in a large, loud room filled with people. It would be inaccurate to say that someone is "partially neurodivergent" because they experience anxiety or have a hard time with sensory stimulation.

- "You can make eye contact. You can't be neurodivergent, right?" Neurodivergence is a diagnosis made by a medical specialist. A medical diagnosis is based on the presence of multiple symptoms that are present in different settings over an extended period of time. A neurodivergent individual will have many of the characteristics associated with the condition, but that does not mean that each neurodivergent person is exactly the same. Every medical condition presents slightly differently because each person is a different combination of genetics and experiences. Neurodiversity is no different in this respect (Cleveland Clinic, 2025e). You cannot disqualify someone from being neurodivergent simply because they do not exhibit one stereotypical characteristic, such as the inability to make eye contact. Remember, stereotypes are often incorrect.

- "Neurodivergence is a mental-health condition like schizophrenia." Autism and many other diagnoses, such as Tourette's syndrome, dyslexia, or ADHD, are not mental-health conditions. They are neurodevelopmental disorders (University of Rochester Medical Center, 2025). This means that they affect how the brain develops and operates. Someone can have a diagnosis of autism, for example, without having a mental health diagnosis such as anxiety or depression. At the same time, since autism affects the way that children interact with others and process emotions, these children are more likely to experience anxiety or depression, especially in social situations.

- "I have to admit, that stuff seems a little too trendy for me. It's not a real diagnosis." There is a great deal of uncertainty about why the prevalence of neurodiversity, particularly autism and ADHD, is increasing. This question is challenging to answer because, like many medical diagnoses, the reasons probably stem from a combination of genetics and environmental factors. As the medical field has evolved, specialists have begun to identify these diagnoses and provide the resources to help neurodivergent individuals be more successful (Moses, 2023). At the same time, environmental factors, such as food quality, medication side effects, or even toxin exposures, are being examined as possible contributing factors to these diagnoses (Dufault et al., 2023). Regardless of the source of the condition, people who are experiencing these diagnoses today need support. Denying the existence of a condition does not support the individuals who may be struggling to be productive members of the classroom or the workforce (Russell, 2020).

- "I know someone who is neurodivergent, and you are nothing like him." Conditions such as autism have often been called *spectrum disorders*, which indicates the variability of the condition from mild to more severe. The medical diagnosis of autism expressed in the *Diagnostic and Statistical Manual of Mental Disorders—Text Revision*, 5th edition (DSM-5-TR) is classified as Type 1 through Type 3 (American Psychiatric Association, 2022). This scale is based on the perceived severity of the condition. No two individuals with autism will have the same visible symptoms, so no one should assume that a child doesn't have autism simply because the child behaves differently than another child with autism.

- "Are you high-functioning or low-functioning?" Despite terminology that indicates more severe cases of conditions such as autism, there has never been medical terminology that specifically states "high functioning" and "low functioning" (Gillette, 2023). The adult autism community and other members of the neurodivergent community have come to find these terms limiting. Also, this terminology attempts to define which characteristics are more important than others. If an individual with a neurodivergent condition struggles with traits such as stimming, masking, emotional dysregulation, communication, and defensive/aggressive behaviors, which of these behaviors is less "functional?" If a child constantly demonstrates stim behaviors, does that mean that they are nonfunctional? Because of these negative stereotypes, the neurodivergent community has moved away from the idea of a linear spectrum and has begun to gravitate toward a definition that looks more like a pie graph, showing the variety of areas that individuals may struggle with or excel at. This type of depiction of the neurodivergent condition allows individuals to see that each person exhibits their condition differently and shows that each individual trait may affect the neurodivergent individual differently.

- "I thought you had to be a genius to be neurodivergent." The media has offered portrayals of neurodivergent individuals that, while popular, are stereotypical depictions. These include Dustin Hoffman's performance of Raymond Babbitt in *Rain Man* and Jim Parsons's comic performance as Dr. Sheldon Cooper in *The Big Bang Theory*. Of course, stereotypes are based on some level of truth, but they do not apply to all individuals. The most common media portrayal of a neurodivergent individual is a genius with significant social or communication delays. Although many neurodivergent children and adults have a difficult time with social communication, not all neurodivergent individuals do. It is also not correct to assume that all neurodivergent individuals are savants. Many neurodivergent people have strong memory skills and a great attention to detail. At the same time, many neurodivergent people may have a medical condition that affects their cognitive development. Media portrayals are fiction. It is essential not to let stereotypes guide the perceptions of neurodiversity.

A Strengths-Based Approach

Instead of focusing solely on deficits, a strengths-based approach to neurodiversity looks more at differences (Vromen, 2023). Each person, neurotypical or neurodivergent, has differences that make that individual unique. Because each person is different, individuals have skills to offer that others may not be able to contribute. At the same time, individuals have challenges that may prevent them from being successful. To be as successful as possible, those individuals need to find supports from teachers, doctors, family, or peers to overcome their challenges.

In the classroom, the same type of theory applies. Each child has areas where they are surpassing the expected developmental milestone for the age, and each child has areas where they need more support to master certain skills. This is why Universal Design for Learning (UDL) has become such a popular concept in the education system, because each child in the classroom needs a customized curriculum based on individualized strengths and challenges, to be as successful as possible (Klonowska and Chen, 2024).

If our education system is going to be set up in a manner to affirm differences, then we must avoid forcing all children to be compliant to a neurotypical setting (Hartman et al., 2024). Neurodiverse children are not going to be successful sitting at a desk all day long and being forced to do math problems using the same algorithm over and over. This is already a challenge for neurotypical children who also need to move and explore to take in new information. It is even more challenging for children who do not think and explore learning in the same manner. One of the greatest challenges in the neurotypical classroom for young children is the social structure of the classroom. When neurodiverse children feel uncomfortable with group play and group projects, teachers try to force them into these settings and penalize them if their social skills don't allow them to align with the expectations. Instead of forcing children into settings that are uncomfortable, we need to be thinking about what works for them, instead of how to change them.

Start with Vocabulary

The language that we use when talking about people who are different from ourselves is reflective of how we feel about those people. When talking about individuals with disabilities, one of the first discussions that often comes up in conversation is people-first language (Woolridge, 2023). People-first language is a way of speaking that acknowledges the person before the disability, making sure that the disability is not the predominant factor that you identify compared to the individual. For example, instead of saying "that epileptic woman," you would refer to the individual as "a woman with epilepsy." The respect is placed on the individual and not the disability, since having seizures is not the defining characteristic for which they want to be known.

A second style of communication would be identity-first language (Woolridge, 2023). In identity-first language, the disability would be the initial description before identifying the person. For example, with identity-first language, you would identify someone as an autistic man instead of saying a man with autism. In most cases, people-first language is preferred throughout the disability community; however, this preference has changed somewhat in the neurodivergent community. There are neurodivergent individuals, especially those in the autism community, who prefer identity-first language (Brown, 2011). Individuals who are promoting identity-first language prefer to be called *autistic* instead of a "person with autism." The reasoning is that their autism is not something that needs to be "cured." They believe autism is part of who they are and makes them unique. Instead of separating themselves from their diagnosis, they are embracing their uniqueness. At the same time, other individuals with autism would still prefer people-first language and appreciate being known for who they are rather than for their diagnosis.

Each individual in the neurodivergent community is going to have a different preference, so the most respectful thing to do to address them in the manner they prefer is simply to ask the individual. Neither way is correct or incorrect. Someone with dyslexia may prefer people-first language, while someone with autism may prefer to be called autistic. The key is to make sure that each individual feels respected within the conversation. This text uses identity-first language since that is the preference of many adult members of the autistic community. Of course, this text focuses on autistic children, but most young children have not yet established a preference for people-first or identity-first language.

Here are some other preferred language choices in the neurodiversity community:

- Using *traits* instead of *red flags*
- Using *special interest* or *deep interest* instead of *obsession*
- Avoid using *high functioning* or *low functioning*

Again, these preferences look at showing respect to all neurodivergent individuals and focusing on strengths instead of deficits.

Identify Benefits

For years, the special education and medical systems have been set up to find deficits and to treat them. In some ways, this approach has been successful. No one wants to go to a doctor who cannot investigate and find an ailment. On the other hand, it is overwhelming to go to specialists and hear nothing but negative news. When you talk to families of children with a diagnosed disability, they will tell you that one of the worst days of the year is when they have to go to school for their child's annual special education meeting to update the child's IEP. The purpose of the meeting is to set achievable goals for the child over the next academic year, but the reality is that parents sit down at a table full of education specialists who all describe the child's educational and behavioral deficits. This large amount of negative information can easily dishearten anyone, and parents often leave feeling hopeless.

Of course, children with disabilities do need supports such as an IEP to be as successful as possible in school; however, instead of focusing on all the aspects of the child that need to be "fixed" or "cured," the goal of this meeting should be to build on the child's strengths and motivate the child based on perceived victories. Some schools have already achieved this new perspective, but as a whole, the infrastructure of the special education system is supposed to identify the problems and attempt to fix the problem in the most efficient manner with the least cost. However, we have seen significant benefits for children, teachers, and families when education programs have focused on neurodiversity-affirming behaviors (Bauer, 2024).

Benefits of Neurodiversity-Affirming Behaviors

Benefits for children:

- Children are more likely to have their individualized education needs met.
- Curriculum based on a child's strengths has helped children increase their confidence.
- Children are less likely to feel judged or inadequate.

Benefits for teachers:

- Teachers are more likely to build stronger relationships with each student when they work to individualize the curriculum.
- The learning approach is more ethical when the curriculum is developed by educational goals instead of diagnosis.
- Teachers experience emotional benefits when they see students making progress and achieving personal goals.

Benefits for families:

- Family members sense that their children are being respected instead of being viewed as a problem that needs to be fixed.
- Family members are more willing to be involved in their children's education when they feel it is a positive experience for the children.

What Is a Neurodiversity-Affirming Classroom?

For years, the predominant treatment of autism and some other neurodivergent conditions included applied behavior analysis (ABA) therapy. This approach has recently received harsh feedback for forcing children to display neurotypical behaviors (Garey, 2024a). At its beginning, this approach sometimes included punishing children for not acquiring "normal" skills. But even today, children are encouraged to repeat the same behaviors to learn to behave "normally" and to eliminate behaviors that are atypical. Of course, in the case of self-injurious behaviors or behaviors could harm others, safety must come first, so children must learn other methods of coping. When safety isn't the issue, it is unnecessary to force neurodivergent children to behave like neurotypical children. A neurodiversity-affirming classroom will allow these children to be themselves, without the harsh mental-health effects of masking (Psychology Today, 2025), and still be included in the learning community.

What are the traits of a classroom that is neurodiversity-affirming?

- Safety is still a top priority, so the education team will work with the child to eliminate self-injurious behaviors or behaviors that could hurt others.
- Children are not required to mask their true behaviors. Stim behaviors and additional movement may be present in the classroom. Children are allowed to pursue their deep interests. If a child is highly motivated by art, for example, then the teacher may encourage the child to use art tools to express what they learned from their last reading assignment.
- The classroom is set up in a way to help children self-regulate with materials such as a calming corner, a movement ball for a seat at a desk, or other tools that can benefit the children's needs. If a child is struggling to self-regulate, then the teacher can show the child appropriate options for self-regulation instead of sending the child to the administrator's office when the child feels overwhelmed.
- The teacher does not assume that certain children are broken or damaged. Instead, the teacher looks at the children's skills and interests to individualize the curriculum.
- The classroom community is designed to respect the way that each child communicates.
- Children are taught how to advocate for their needs, and the teachers listen when a child says that they have a specific need.
- Much like Maria Montessori's classroom structure, the classroom is child led. That does not mean that children set all of the rules. Instead, the children's interests can guide the learning to help them be more engaged and invested.

Supporting Children Through Challenges

Even in inclusive and welcoming classrooms, children will have challenging days or even weeks. The key in a neurodiversity-affirming classroom is for the teacher to continue to offer support to the child during the challenging times and to help find solutions that fit the individual child. Knowing that a preschool classroom may have twenty-plus students, and an elementary school classroom could have up to thirty students, teachers expect that there will be multiple children in their classroom each year who have a variety of special needs. Those could be diagnosed disabilities, chronic health conditions, or children dealing with trauma. No matter the children's backgrounds, the teacher must find a way to develop a relationship with each child and meet their individual needs. The first step to identifying a child's needs is to know the child. Once the child trusts the teacher, that child is much more likely to let the teacher know what is going on. Also, if the teacher knows a child well, the teacher may not even need the child to explain what the problem is because the teacher may already be picking up on the child's cues. This relationship is essential for trust, and trust is what will allow the children to be vulnerable and attempt to overcome their challenges.

Accommodations

Every child in a classroom needs some type of accommodation. Some children may have a legal document such as an IEP or a 504 Plan due to a disability or a health condition, but other children may still need simple accommodations to be their best selves (Pillai and Branch, 2023). For example, a student may start to lose focus each day in the late morning simply because they metabolize their breakfast faster than others and need a snack to keep their body running until lunchtime. It is typically an easy accommodation to allow a student to bring snacks from home to keep at school.

The teacher might consider offering an accommodation to the whole class; doing so can have multiple benefits. First, if everyone can use an accommodation, such as a morning snack, that doesn't alienate one student and make them feel different from the rest. Second, if one student needs that accommodation, there is a strong chance that they are not the only child in the classroom who would benefit from that accommodation.

The goal of accommodations is to give the child the best chance to be successful without making the child feel different from every other child. In preschool and early elementary school, children may not be as worried about seeming different from peers, but as children get closer to adolescence, they need to feel like a member of the classroom community instead of an outsider. Remember, it isn't only children with special education support who may need accommodations.

If a child is struggling with a concept or with a component of the classroom environment, then it is worth evaluating whether something needs to change to support that child. Sometimes, children just need a little more time in a consistent environment to be successful. But on other occasions, the teacher needs to be willing to change methods for the sake of the children.

Bullying

When neurodiverse children are in traditional classroom settings, their differences can stand out. Being in a setting that highlights these differences can lead to classroom peers bullying neurodivergent students (Alcorn et al., 2024). In contrast, research studies have shown that using the following methods can create more inclusive and welcoming classrooms (Soldovieri, 2024).

- Establish a neurodiversity-affirming classroom that celebrates each student's strengths and allows children to meet their own needs. Doing so shows that the school and the teacher are supporting the differences of all the children.
- Make accommodations not only for the neurodivergent children but for every child in the classroom. This approach encourages each student to be more like their true selves.
- Provide age-appropriate education to the students about neurodiversity. Doing so can decrease incidences of bullying. If the students understand and respect each other, then the sense of community will grow.

Self-Acceptance

Another benefit of a strengths-based, neurodiversity-affirming classroom is that children begin to develop more self-confidence than in settings where children have to mask neurodiverse behaviors during the school day (Psychology Today, 2025). When a respected adult, such as a teacher, accepts each child's behavior, then children seem more willing to accept their own behaviors. Self-acceptance is an advanced skill that many adults have still not acquired, but laying a foundation in early childhood can help children learn to accept themselves as a whole much sooner than if they are in an environment where their behaviors are questioned and criticized.

To provide necessary accommodations and improve the overall mental health of many neurodivergent children in inclusive classroom settings, this book examines strategies that are not used in typical preschool and elementary school settings. These techniques are in alignment with national educational standards; however, instead of relying on a curriculum that has children focus strictly on reading, writing, and math, these techniques will support children's deep interests and build engagement and self-confidence. Although the strategies may be nontraditional, the neurodiversity-affirming classrooms that use these techniques still have the ability to include all children and meet the academic goals of each student enrolled. One of the first approaches to creating a comfortable classroom for neurodiverse children is to create a sensory-friendly classroom that will benefit all students.

CHAPTER 3:

The Sensory-Friendly Classroom

Once teachers and families have a greater understanding of neurodivergent conditions, then it is possible to start planning classroom supports and strategies. Jean Piaget created one of the most esteemed theories on child development (Rabindran, 2020). Piaget was a stage theorist, meaning that he believed that human development moves through stages based on age and developmental maturity. The first stage of development is called *sensorimotor development*. Piaget believed that as soon as young children begin to develop their motor skills, they use those skills—reaching, crawling, walking, climbing—to gather sensory information from their environments. To learn about the world, a child needs to be able to see it, taste it, touch it, and hear it (McLeod, 2024). Gathering and interpreting sensory information is what allows children to move on to higher stages of learning.

Even after the toddler years, sensory information is still incredibly important to the learning process. As young children, students are taught that each person has five senses: sight, hearing, touch, taste, and smell. When it comes to human development, there are actually eight senses that are critical for the learning experience. The three additional senses include the proprioceptive sense, the vestibular sense, and the interoceptive sense.

The *proprioceptive sense* is responsible for body awareness and the ability to feel the body move through space (Dahlerbruch, 2022). This sense allows someone to walk through a room without bumping into the furniture and walls. Proprioception also allows a person to use the right amount of energy for the task at hand or to exert the correct amount of force to use a hammer. One of the main purposes of proprioceptive information is to calm the nervous system enough to organize the mind and body. A child with difficulty processing proprioceptive information is going to have an extremely difficult time self-regulating.

The *vestibular sense* is responsible for balance, with the help of the inner ear (Murphy, 2024). Again, this system feels the body move through space, but its response is to find where the body is in space and to stabilize it. When a child is on a playground swing or riding a bike, the vestibular sense helps the body understand where the body is positioned and how to balance and remain upright. The major gross motor skills, such as crawling, standing, and walking, are dependent upon the vestibular sense. When the vestibular sense is not functioning properly, then the child will have poor posture, poor eye-hand coordination, and an inability to balance.

Finally, the *interoceptive sense* is responsible for helping our body to connect to what we are feeling and to understand those feelings such as thirst, hunger, pain, and illness (Sharman, 2022). Interception also allows the body to connect with the emotions that the brain is feeling. When children are first born, they are overreactive to what they feel, such as screaming every time they are hungry or tired. As they mature, children begin to be able to express their needs without emotional outbursts; some emotions, however, are still so big that children may still have strong reactions when they experience them. For example, when preschool or school-age children are exhausted, they may begin to cry and overreact to the simplest complication. They are not aware of how desperately their body needs sleep. When a child struggles with the interoceptive sense, they may consistently have "big emotions," even when the emotions are not proportionate to the situation. An under-responsive interoceptive sense may prevent a child from identifying when they feel pain or illness. For a child to develop fully, all eight senses must be working effectively.

What Is a Sensory-Friendly Classroom?

A sensory-friendly classroom is a classroom that accommodates the sensory needs of every child in the space (Child Mind Institute, 2024). This model acknowledges that the traditional classroom environment of brightly colored walls with rows of desks facing the teacher does not meet the needs of all students, and in some cases, it makes it much harder for children to learn. The traditional learning model relies on children sitting in desks and ingesting most of the educational content by looking and listening. Children who have additional sensory needs, particularly a need for movement during the school day, can struggle with this model. A teacher in a sensory-friendly classroom will adjust the classroom design and behavior-management techniques to benefit all the children, instead of just those students who learn by seeing and listening.

One of the major goals of the sensory-friendly classroom is to support children who experience *sensory processing dysfunction*, a condition in which the brain has a difficult time processing the information that is collected through the child's senses (Goodman, 2023). As we discuss in chapter 1, sensory processing dysfunction is not a medical condition but a symptom experienced by many children and adults who are neurodivergent. Some neurotypical individuals also experience some levels of sensory processing dysfunction. A classroom that can accommodate the diverse sensory needs of many different children can ensure that both neurodivergent and neurotypical children have the sensory environment they need to be successful.

The Benefits of a Sensory-Friendly Classroom

Traditional preschool and elementary school classrooms are often depicted in the media. Filled with an explosion of color and artwork hanging from the ceiling, twenty-five small voices all talk at the same time. Inevitably, at least one child is crying, and it is easy to imagine that the classroom smells like tempera paint and school glue. Most adults are overwhelmed with the idea of entering this classroom, but imagine the task of trying to be productive in this setting on a daily basis. That is a challenge for the most well-regulated child. For a child who is constantly overwhelmed by noise, chaos, and even their own emotions, expecting them to excel in this environment is unreasonable.

A sensory-friendly classroom, on the other hand, has several distinct benefits that can help all children be more successful (Fisher, 2024).

- **Reduced anxiety:** A calm, structured classroom without overstimulation can significantly reduce anxiety for children who worry about going to school each day.
- **Increased participation:** Children who are not constantly distracted by their environment are much more likely to participate in group conversations and finish independent work assignments.
- **Increased concentration:** It is much easier for a child to focus on their work and learn the classroom content when they are not worried about flickering fluorescent lights, the sharp buzz of an electric pencil sharpener, or trying to sit still throughout a group activity.

- **Improved academic performance:** When children can focus on schoolwork and are engaged in school activities, doing so naturally affects their academic performance (or preacademic performance for preschoolers).
- **Improved self-regulation:** A child who is in a constantly overwhelmed state is simply trying to survive the school day and is not in a place where they can learn new concepts (Morin, 2024). When the sensory stimuli in the classroom are not overwhelming to the student, then it is possible to teach coping skills one at a time and allow the child to use those new skills when they do become overwhelmed.
- **Increased acceptance:** When a classroom is designed to meet the needs of all students, then no particular student stands out as more "different" than another. An inclusive classroom sets a foundation that allows for acceptance and friendships (Stearns, 2022).

The Sensory-Friendly Classroom and the Neurodivergent Mind

Many neurodivergent individuals struggle with sensory processing. These struggles can contribute to how a neurodivergent individual deals with daily events such as transitions or why they have a limited diet. However, it is also important to remember that each individual—whether neurodiverse or neurotypical—has a different sensory profile, so each person has different sensory preferences (Krauss, 2024). With that in mind, a classroom that includes sensory accommodations for each child allows for every student to be more successful. A teacher can begin with establishing consistent routines and reducing unnecessary sensory stimuli in the classroom for the group of children as a whole. Then, when a neurodivergent student needs additional accommodations, supporting that child will not be so difficult.

The Needs of the Sensory-Friendly Classroom

Children's sensory needs may vary. One child may crave additional sensory input, and another may be defensive to that sensory information. Implementing certain concepts at the classroom level and making other accommodations for individual children can help everyone be as successful as possible. These following general classroom strategies will benefit all children— those who are typically developing and those who are neurodivergent (Stearns, 2022):

- Consistent daily routine
- Movement
- Choices
- Balance of experiences
- Sensory information

Consistent Daily Routine

Ensure that children follow a consistent routine. A routine is different from a schedule that says the specific times that events will occur each day. A routine is the order of events. For example, first a child will hang up their coat, wash their hands, and then have breakfast. The order of daily events helps children feel secure because they know what is coming next. Even when the time of events must change, it is important to keep the *order* of classroom events consistent.

Movement

Make sure that lessons are an appropriate length for the age children in the classroom, and allow movement between learning opportunities. Due to increasing academic pressure (even in preschool) teachers have begun teaching longer, direct lessons to young children. The length of time a child can sit still and focus is short, and asking children to keep their bodies still and engage with the teacher for an extended amount of time can cause a great deal of stress. Young children learn through movement and exploration, so teachers should design the classroom to support that learning method. We will take a deeper look at the benefits of dance in chapter 6.

Choices

Give children choices. When children only have one choice such as, "Everyone is going to fingerpaint now," they can experience strong sensory reactions and can have big emotions. On the other hand, when children have options such as, "You can sit on your carpet square, or you can sit behind the rest of the class to have more room to move," they can make the best possible decision for themselves while still participating in the activity.

Allow a child the opportunity to decline an activity or situation that could be overwhelming. While teachers often allow children to decline activities that are extremely loud and chaotic, it is also important to allow children the opportunity to decline situations that may seem minor. Trying a new food, fingerpainting, or walking on grass barefoot can be just as overwhelming for some children as a large school assembly. When a child seems genuinely concerned about a new experience, the teacher should give the child the option to participate but accept the child's preference not to.

Balance of Experiences

Offer a balance of experiences and activities: loud and quiet, group and individual, indoor and outdoor, and so on. Offer opportunities that support children with different learning styles: visual, auditory, and kinesthetic. Visual cues can be just as important as giving auditory instructions. Allow children to learn by doing so kinesthetic learners have extra opportunities for hands-on learning and movement.

Sensory Information

Individual children may seek or defend against specific sensory information. In those cases, the teacher may need to adapt the classroom as a whole (depending on how significant a child's needs are) or may need to alter an activity for a specific child. In these cases, it is important to look at the specific sensory system that affects the child and whether the child needs more input or less. Depending on whether the children need more or less sensory information, here is a possible list of strategies than can support them:

- **Visual Seeking**
    - Offer toys such as view finders, kaleidoscopes, or I Spy books for extra visual stimulation.
    - Use color-changing lights or optical illusions.
- **Visual Defensive**
    - Keep the classroom free of clutter or stacks of materials.
    - Use a calmer classroom aesthetic without something hung on every wall space.
    - Cover or dim lights.
- **Auditory Seeking**
    - Have the child listen to someone read aloud.
    - Play music during free play or independent work time.
    - Encourage the child to play with toys that make noise

- **Auditory Defensive**
  - Provide the children with noise-reducing headphones when the environment is too loud.
  - Warn the child before very loud activities such as a fire drill.
- **Olfactory Seeking**
  - Use scented playdough, markers, or stickers.
  - If possible, do baking activities in the classroom so the child can experience different aromas.
- **Olfactory Defensive**
  - Avoid wearing strong perfumes or scented personal-care products.
  - Find classroom cleaning products without strong odors that could cause the child distress.
- **Tactile Seeking**
  - Use slimes, putties, and touch-and-feel books for different sensory stimulation.
  - Incorporate sensory boxes and regularly change the contents.
- **Tactile Defensive**
  - Modify art activities to lessen the sensory experience. For example, provide a brush for the child to use when the rest of the class is fingerpainting, or provide tools with playdough.
  - Work with the family to provide meal options that the child is willing to eat, or the child could brush his teeth before the meal to desensitize the mouth before trying different food textures.
  - Allow the child to stand at the front or back of the line so they don't have someone bumping into them on both sides and can take an extra amount of personal space.
- **Taste Seeking**
  - Offer foods with intense flavors, such as lemon wedges or salsa (with chips), that the child can take when needing the extra sensory information.
  - Offer crunchy foods for snack time such as carrot sticks and pretzels to offer a different sensory experience.
  - Provide appropriate items for the child to chew on, such as chewy bracelets or necklaces, so the child doesn't chew on his clothing and classroom materials.

- **Taste Defensive**
  - Offer water in between different foods, so the child isn't overwhelmed by many different tastes at once.
  - Create a game with rewards for trying new foods (but don't have it at meal time: use it doing normal classroom free time).
  - Use minimal seasoning for foods prepared at school.
- **Proprioceptive Seeking**
  - Incorporate deep pressure activities. Find ways to include deep pressure activities into the classroom day, so the child's central nervous system gets the necessary information it needs to organize itself.
  - Increase movement. Make sure that children have the opportunity to be active throughout the day, even when completing school work.
- **Proprioceptive Defensive**
  - Focus on calming movement activities, instead of those that burn energy.
  - When a child says that an activity is too much, listen. The child should be considered the expert.
- **Vestibular Seeking**
  - Use indoor and outdoor obstacle courses to master balance.
  - Use tools such as trampolines and rocking chairs to practice bouncing, swinging, and back and forth movements.
- **Vestibular Defensive**
  - Don't force the child to participate in activities that are "too much."
  - When doing movement activities, consider calm movements that move in only one direction.
- **Interoceptive**
  - Breathing activities
  - Mindfulness activities

Classroom Activities

Both preschool and elementary school classrooms need to plan activities that ensure all children receive the sensory experiences they need. Some of these activities should be integrated into the curriculum to support whole-child development. Other activities may be based on what a child needs to self-regulate his behavior. For example, a child requiring additional sensory input might help create the classroom bulletin boards, so they can bang the stapler against the bulletin-board wall and receive that extra sensory information. Remember Piaget's development theory that all children learn by seeking sensory information. Every child in the classroom needs access to some sensory experiences to grow and develop fully. The following is a list of potential activities and tools that can be available to the entire classroom or to children who need those extra experiences:

- **Playdough and slime:** Playdough and slime allow children to have different tactile experiences. They also allow children to use a variety of energy levels to move and sculpt the clay, when a child may need a deep pressure experience to calm the emotions.
- **Sensory obstacle courses:** This can be a small obstacle course through the room or down the hallway that allows children to experience different textures. For example, children can take their shoes off and walk on the cold tile, then onto a carpet square, over a cardboard box, and across an egg-crate mattress. A wide range of surfaces can be used for this tactile experience.
- **Small trampoline:** An individual trampoline lets one child expend a huge amount of energy while providing lots of vestibular input as the child moves through space and balances his body.
- **Essential oils:** For additional olfactory stimulation, use an essential oil diffuser. The teacher can select scents that help calm a child's nervous system.
- **Sensory bins:** A water table is often large, so it can be costly to place a variety of materials in it. A small plastic bin (the size of a shoe box) can be used to expose children to a wide variety of sensory experiences, such as dry rice, shaving cream, kinetic sand, or smooth, cold stones. Be sure to change the contents of these boxes regularly to provide a variety of experiences. You can also hide small charms or beads in the bins so children will have to dig through the entire bin to find the hidden objects. Because many children will use the same activity, be sure that children wash their hands before and after using the bins.
- **Sensory jars (or calm-down jars):** Sensory jars can be a wonderful classroom activity and are easy to make. They can contain a variety of items such as water, glitter, food coloring, and baby or vegetable oil. Depending on the theme of the bottle, you could add items such as seashells, beads, or small plastic toys. Place the items in plastic jars or bottles to make sure that they do not break when a child drops them, and hot glue the tops of the jars on so a child cannot easily take the top off. The calm-down jar encourages the child to shake the bottle with all of their strength, then watch as all the items inside slowly settle. This activity allows

children to use energetic and aggressive movements, as well as slow and calming movements.

- **Smelling jars:** Some children are more sensitive to smells than others, and these children may easily become overwhelmed in a classroom full of active, young bodies. To provide a positive olfactory experience, the teacher can create smelling jars with baby-food jars or similar, cotton balls, and scented oils. Pour a small amount of the scented oil onto the cotton ball and place it inside the jar. Poke holes in the top of the jar so the student can smell the scent without taking off the lid. Some popular scents include peppermint, lavender, or lemon. The teacher can personalize the activity based on the needs of the students.
- **Water play:** Water play can be available in a water table or in a plastic tub on the classroom floor. Water should be changed out multiple times per day, and children should wash their hands before and after participating. Add food coloring to dye the water different colors, and add toys to scoop and move the water. Water play should always be supervised because even a couple of inches (a few centimeters) of standing water can be a drowning risk.
- **Bubble-wrap stomping:** This is an easy activity for the classroom in which all children—and adults—love to participate. They can pop bubble wrap with their fingers, but if they need a larger amount of pressure, they can stomp on it. Teachers can ask parents to donate bubble wrap after they have packages delivered. Because this activity can be loud, warn students who are sensitive to loud noises. They may want to wear noise-reducing headphones while their classmates pop bubbles.
- **Textured art:** Because preschool and early elementary art should be focused on the process rather than the product, providing a variety of different textures fits into that philosophy. Paint can be altered by mixing it with sand, liquid soap, shaving cream, or water. The experience of spreading the paint on the paper changes as the texture changes. You can read more about art activities in chapter 8.
- **Weighted lap pads or weighted blankets:** For children who crave deep pressure to calm down and self-regulate, weighted lap pads and blankets can be an asset. It is important for the teacher to order the appropriately weighted blanket. Follow guidelines on how heavy a blanket should be based on the weight of the child. Do not order a blanket that is meant for an adult weight. A blanket that is too heavy can make it hard for the child to take deep breaths or can make the child feel as if they are suffocating.
- **Fidget toys:** Teachers can keep a box of fidget toys in the classroom for children to use when they need additional tactile experiences or need to move part of their body to focus. Most fidget toys, such as pop toys, bendy toys, or squeeze toys that have a variety of textures, allow for continuous movement.

- **Noise-canceling headphones:** For children who are often overwhelmed by the sounds of a busy classroom (or school assemblies), noise-canceling headphones can be extremely helpful. Make sure they are the appropriate size for the children in the classroom. If the headphones are too big, they will not stay on effectively to block additional noise.
- **Bear hugs and hand hugs:** Some children seek deep pressure to self-regulate their nervous system. Bear hugs or hand hugs can be a way to offer that deep pressure. The teacher can offer the child a bear hug to help calm down. If the child needs more of a sense of control, then the child can bear hug the teacher. Some children may not want their whole body to be hugged, so hand hugs may offer them some sense of deep pressure.
- **Alternative seating:** Although most classrooms are set up with desks and chairs, many children learn better in a variety of positions. Teachers can use floor pillows, wobble seats, yoga balls, and standing desks to help children participate in the learning environment and still receive the movement they need.
- **Preferential seating:** Sitting next to doors, windows, or even certain peers can be distracting for some students. A teacher may need to place certain students in areas of the room where they are able to concentrate better without feeling alienated. This can be a discussion between the child and the teacher to decide where the best seat may be.
- **Classroom hiding place:** Each classroom should have a place where a child can find solitude when they are overwhelmed by the sensory information around them. This can decrease behavior problems once a child understands that they just need to be alone instead of taking out their frustration on a friend. Some classrooms have small tents or large decorated cardboard boxes that children can retreat to when they are overwhelmed. Other classrooms may just need to pick an area that feels safe for the individual child. For instance, a child might hide under the teacher's desk until they are ready to rejoin the group.
- **Sit 'n Spins and rocking chairs:** Much like a personal trampoline, a Sit 'n Spin or a rocking chair provides additional vestibular input for students who need it. They are safer than allowing students to jump off tables or playground equipment.
- **Heaving lifting:** Heavy lifting can be beneficial for students who need deep pressure. They can carry books or supplies to another part of the classroom or carry the emergency backpack to the playground for recess.
- **Swinging on the playground:** Although many swings have been removed from school playgrounds, they are one of the best sources of vestibular input for young children. Many occupational therapists have a therapy swing in their office that can be used for self-regulation, if the school therapist has an office on the school campus.

- **Classroom set-up and clean-up:** When a teacher is looking for unique ways to offer heavy lifting to children who need help self-regulating, the beginning- and end-of-the-day routines can be beneficial. Stacking chairs on top of desks, carrying out the trash, and a variety of daily routines can offer that heavy lifting input.
- **Furniture adjustments:** Classroom furniture should be suited to the size of the children to support their sensory needs. If the chairs are too tall, then the children's feet may swing back and forth and constantly create distracting sensory information. Inappropriate sizing can also make handwriting difficult when a child has to reach farther than is comfortable.
- **Appropriate chew items:** Some children constantly put objects into their mouths and chew on items such as their fingernails or pencils and other classroom materials. Instead of worrying about what they chew on, find appropriate items for them to use, such as a chewing necklace the child can wear and or therapy tubing tied into a necklace. Older children may be able to chew gum responsibly during class (with parent permission).
- **Morning calisthenics:** All students can benefit by starting the day with movement. A brief session of simple exercises (or yoga) can meet the children's movement needs and help everyone focus afterward.
- **Movement breaks:** Even in elementary school, teachers must ensure that children are not seated for too long at one time. The brain is designed in a way that children want to move and seek out knowledge, not just sit and listen. Some children need even more movement because they are natural kinesthetic learners. In this case, the teacher may need to find additional movement breaks for the child throughout the day, such as asking them to do an errand or deliver materials to a peer on the other side of the classroom.
- **Structured playground time:** Although many teachers covet playground time to have a little time to themselves, a structured playground time can often help students get the movement they need. Many students may not be active on the playground and use the time to socialize instead. Although socializing is also important, there may be days when the class really needs to release energy. Just like with morning calisthenics, the teacher can guide the class through a variety of activities. While outside, there is more room to use activities such as bear crawls, crab walks, frog hops, and other large motor activities.
- **Daily classroom quiet time:** Each day should have a small amount of quiet time so students have an auditory break. This can be silent reading in elementary school or nap time in preschool. However it is planned into the schedule, students should have the option for an auditory break.

Challenges of the Sensory-Friendly Classroom

One of the greatest challenges of the sensory-friendly classroom is supporting two children who have opposite sensory needs. For example, some children may be seeking additional visual stimuli. These children may benefit from computer programs that use additional lights or brightly colored activities. A child with epilepsy who has photo-sensitive seizures, on the other hand, might experience a seizure induced by the lights on the computer. In these settings, it is best to set up the overall classroom based on safety guidelines or necessary medical advice for the child with these specific needs. Then, the teacher can provide additional sensory activities for the one child who is seeking additional visual stimuli.

Another challenge of the sensory-friendly classroom can be convincing administrators and more traditional teachers that nontraditional teaching styles can benefit the learning environment (Ayres, 2023). Consider, for example, a teacher who requires all students to sit during seat work and becomes frustrated when a student stands up and sways back and forth while completing assignments. Some teachers were trained that this child is distracting the rest of the class and needs to sit while working to be respectful. Unfortunately, when asked to sit, the child may be constantly distracted by his need to move.

Every teacher wants their students to be successful, so many are willing to change if the problem is clearly identified and a viable solution is presented. Techniques such as nontraditional seating can be appealing if teachers see that the solution will work. Inviting teachers to observe a classroom where new techniques have been successfully implemented can be helpful. Teachers also may be more open to change if they learn to identify the behavior problems and triggers that are occurring for multiple students in the classroom. Sometimes, a fellow teacher or an administrator can assist with identifying these problems with a classroom observation. Other times, a special-education teacher or an occupational therapist might give a classroom consultation on how to support students who are struggling. With documented data, many teachers are willing to change their strategies.

Another aspect of classroom sensory information can be the aesthetic design of the space. Aesthetics continues to focus on the visual stimulation of the classroom but has more to do with pleasing visuals and a warm environment. We will explore this more in the following chapter.

CHAPTER 4:
Aesthetics in the Early Childhood Classroom

After taking a look at how a sensory-friendly classroom can have an effect on neurodivergent children, it is also helpful to consider how the classroom design affects the child's ability to function. When teachers design their classroom, they engage in a personal experience because many aspects of the design directly reflect their personalities. At the same time, they may not be aware of small design decisions that can influence behavior and performance. Both the Montessori approach and the Reggio Emilia approach regard the classroom as the "third teacher," so with that in mind, the classroom must be as prepared as possible to serve a wide variety of students (American Montessori Society, 2024; Reggio Emilia Early Learning Centre, 2023).

What Is a Classroom Aesthetic?

The classroom aesthetic is the visual appearance and design of the classroom, including elements such as lighting, colors, furniture arrangement, and the classroom atmosphere as a whole. These factors can affect the energy level of the children, their engagement in classroom activities, and how comfortable they feel in moving around the room. One of the major goals of an early childhood classroom (both preschool and elementary school) is for children to be curious in the environment. This curiosity encourages children to explore the classroom materials, try new activities, and be excited about what they can learn (Ward, 2009). When children are trying new things and exploring, they are thinking and asking how and why something works, which is the basis of the scientific method for learning (Worth, 2010). The environment itself is part of this learning process, so it should be designed to support the learners.

Reggio Emilia–inspired design principles include some of the following ideas (Devi, 2022):

1. Creating a community focus to foster relationships, communication, and curriculum development
2. Using transparency in the environment through indirect and natural lighting and transparent materials
3. Including natural and authentic materials
4. Bringing the outside into the classroom to create areas of natural beauty
5. Providing dedicated spaces to minimize transitions and allow children's building and exploration to continue over a sustained period
6. Using pedagogical documentation to capture children's messages about their classroom environment and to understand deeply their learning experiences, theories, and ways of knowing

Much like the principles in the sensory-friendly classroom, many of the Reggio Emilia principles on classroom design contrast with the images of preschool and elementary school classrooms that are depicted in media or that many adults remember from their childhood.

What Are the Components of Classroom Aesthetics?

Each classroom design is composed of many different parts, so it is important to understand the complexity of the design. The following components create a beautiful classroom environment that allows children to learn in a safe and nurturing classroom setting without overwhelming distractions.

Lighting

Lighting can have a huge effect on the mood of the children and their overall learning (Joanna, 2023). When a classroom is properly lit, it displays the classroom in a positive manner. Also, low levels of light can affect the energy level of the children. Natural light (sunlight shining through windows) can influence the mental and physical health of the children in the classroom.

Classrooms commonly have ceiling lights with long fluorescent light bulbs. These lights are notorious for flickering and buzzing during use. To reduce the harsh glare they emit, many teachers will order light covers that can be placed over them. Other teachers simply keep the overhead lights turned off and use natural light and lamps to light the classroom.

Layout

The layout of a classroom has several major purposes (Joanna, 2023). It needs to ensure that all children are safe and that teachers can supervise each child easily. The layout should allow for children to have social interaction in certain areas of the room, as well as allow each child to have their own personal space. Materials and activities should be visible to children as they move through the classroom, so they are drawn to interesting materials. Also, it is important for the layout separate quieter areas of the classroom from high-traffic areas, so social activities do not disturb activities that require more concentration. Many neurodivergent children crave an organized classroom setting with a reduced amount of sensory information.

Flooring

The classroom flooring has a few important purposes (Joanna, 2023). First, it needs to make sure that children stay safe, so it shouldn't be too slippery or so hard that children are hurt when they fall. Second, the flooring needs to have appropriate acoustics. When flooring causes sound to echo throughout the classroom, children can be overwhelmed with auditory sensory information. This can overwhelm even the children who are not sensory defensive, since a classroom is already an active place. Flooring also contributes to the overall beauty and visual aesthetic in the classroom, so it is preferable that it is not too brightly colored but has a more neutral tone.

Furniture

The classroom furniture needs to make learning accessible for the children (Joanna, 2023). This means that it needs to be appropriately sized for the children who use it. This is essential for neurodivergent children who struggle with balance and other motor skills. When children can't independently access the classroom materials because the shelving is too high or their feet don't touch the floor when they sit in the chairs, then their access to the classroom is naturally limited. Shelving should showcase the classroom materials, not take the attention away from them. Neutral colors for shelving and seating are preferable so they do not distract from classroom learning activities. The seating should not only be sized appropriately for the children but should also be comfortable, so the children can engage in an activity as long as they are interested.

Plants

Even though many teachers may feel that they do not have a green thumb, having plants in the classroom can be beneficial for young children. Plants are beautiful and have some ability to improve indoor air quality (NASA Spinoff, 2019). Further, by helping to water plants, children can learn how to care for another living thing. Because neurodivergent children often struggle with social relationships, they can benefit from learning to care for plants (Anixter and Kelly, 2023).

Color

Exposure to color can have a tremendous effect on human emotion and energy level (London Image Institute, 2020). Natural colors such as cool blues and greens are preferred, with natural wood for shelving and other furniture. Because the early childhood classroom is already energetic, many classroom-design experts will encourage teachers to use cool, neutral colors to help establish a sense of calm and relaxation for the children. The classroom also needs to be welcoming, so a color palette with a few different colors can enhance beauty.

Temperature

The classroom aesthetic also includes the temperature. A research study done in 2018 showed that heat increases as small as one degree could have an effect on student learning and productivity (Goodman, Hurwitz, Park, and Smith, 2018). It is important to have a cool and comfortable classroom to optimize learning.

Proximity and Flow

Proximity and *flow* refer to how close together similar materials may be and how one area of the classroom leads into another curriculum area (Devi, 2022). Some design specialists think of this principle as the "zones" of the classroom. Teachers may closely position classroom construction materials alongside other fine motor activities that could be incorporated into similar play. They could locate collaborative play activities in a similar area of the classroom while keeping individual activities in a separate zone. Children will have the opportunity to blend similar learning materials that are in close proximity to extend learning.

Open-Ended and Closed-Ended Materials

Within the classroom, there should be some materials that have a specific purpose and rules for how to use them. These would be considered closed-ended materials. The classroom should also have a variety of open-ended materials that can be used according to the child's imagination, including materials in the dramatic play area of the classroom, the block and construction area, and most of the art materials (Devi, 2022). Teachers can model the appropriate way to use art media, such as using it on paper and cleaning brushes after use, but leave the subject and form to the children's imaginations. Similarly, there would be some rules in the block area: throwing a block is not allowed, but how the children choose to build is up to them. This spectrum of materials with rules and activities that allow creative freedom is necessary to help children learn both to follow directions and to imagine and create.

The Benefits of Aesthetics in the Early Childhood Classroom

The greatest benefit of designing a classroom aesthetic is that it makes learning a pleasurable and interesting experience (Terada and Merrill, 2023). So many children (and adults) have had negative school experiences that relate back to an issue with the classroom environment. Some children do not want to attend school due to the overwhelming sensory experience of a busy classroom. Others feel that their classroom is dark and uninviting. Some children feel that they don't have enough personal space in the classroom and that there is nowhere to go to be alone when they need time to themselves. All of these negative reactions can be corrected with a properly designed classroom.

Another benefit of classroom aesthetics is that they create a calming environment (Russell, 2019). For neurodivergent children who already struggle with regulating their emotions, a calm environment can help a child learn how to mirror the same level of energy. Once a child is maintaining a lower level of emotional energy, then they are able to engage in classroom activities and focus for a longer period of time.

Aesthetics and the Neurodivergent Mind

What do neurodivergent children need from their classroom environment? Barbara Uherek-Bradecka (2020), an early childhood researcher, specifically looked at this question and found certain characteristics that benefit neurodivergent children in early childhood classrooms. Her list included:

- A sense of peace and order in space
- Adequate level of sunshine and ventilation
- Reduction of too much visual stimulation
- Proper proportions
- Proxemics (the suitable amount of space between people that they consider necessary)
- Stopping of intruders (making sure that people are safe in their environment)
- Materials that are durable and easy to maintain
- Good observation
- Good acoustics

She also asserted that neurodivergent children prefer these factors; they are not just factors that benefit them (Uherek-Bradecka, 2020). Children desire to be in a classroom environment that has limited sensory stimulation but allows for natural light. They want to feel safe when coming to school, and they desire to have their own personal space. They want to be able to observe the classroom as a whole, and they want to hear what is happening throughout the room without being overwhelmed by sound.

These classroom components not only align with the principles of classroom aesthetics, but the design components make the environment sensory-friendly while still encouraging children to learn. This type of learning environment benefits children with atypical abilities, but it also benefits all children. Since it is designed to be inclusive, individual differences do not stand out or need accommodations that other children may not need.

Classroom Aesthetic Reminders

Although designing the perfect classroom aesthetic is largely based on the components listed earlier in this chapter, it is helpful for teachers to keep these reminders in mind while setting up their classroom.

The purpose of creating the classroom aesthetic is to create beauty but not visual distraction. The teacher's goal should be to find a balance between engaging and calming (Wideman-van der Laan, 2023). Children should be able to see their own artwork displayed throughout the classroom, but there should not be so much artwork that it takes over the room. Focus on one or two areas where artwork can be displayed.

Classroom layout should be broken up enough that it prevents children from running around in circles, but there should be enough flow that children can easily move from one zone of the classroom to another. Also, classroom pathways should be clear enough that children with different levels of mobility can still move through the room.

Focus classroom decorations on the children's artwork and professional artwork. Store-bought posters and bulletin board decorations are often cartoonish and lack a realistic look. Cartoonish images can often influence a child's artwork, which is why classic works of art are some of the best models to display. Avoid trademark images in classroom décor. Children are already exposed to a variety of marketing campaigns and cartoon characters. There is nothing wrong with a child's favorite cartoon characters, but the learning environment should offer lots of open-ended experiences. Instead of a trademarked cartoon cat, children should have the opportunity to dream about and draw the cat that they envision, not just the one on a television show.

Think of ways to reduce classroom clutter such as stacking up materials and creating piles. One of the key elements of creating a beautiful learning environment is daily cleaning. This means keeping the classroom clean and sanitized, but it also means taking time each day to put things back into their specific place so clutter does not accumulate.

Part of a well-planned classroom aesthetic includes having a structured daily routine, so children know what to expect each day. Having a visual schedule can reinforce the routine. The schedule should be placed in an area of the classroom where children can easily see it from different areas of the room. Have a dedicated space for classroom activities so children know where to find them and have enough room to complete those activities. When children don't feel that they can access the necessary space to complete an activity, they are much less likely to engage.

Challenges of Creating a Classroom Aesthetic

One of the greatest challenges to creating a beneficial classroom aesthetic is cost. Items such as furniture, lighting, and flooring are expensive and require funding from the school to replace. Knowing that classroom budgets are limited, sometimes teachers must start with elements of the aesthetic over which they have more control. Teachers have the ability to minimize clutter and design a classroom floor plan without a classroom budget. Other changes, such as repainting the classroom walls, may be a small enough expense that the school can support the teacher. Many of the essentials for the classroom design are organizational and not dependent on new materials including:

- Having a structured routine
- Creating zones and flow with classroom layout
- Limiting visual distractions
- Balancing open-ended and closed-ended materials
- Making sure that children have a balance of social interaction and personal space
- Bringing nature into the classroom
- Encouraging curiosity

Teachers can still talk to administrators about long-term goals for the classroom and try to find ways to implement some of the more expensive changes. The important thing to remember is that the classroom design can change even without funding.

One of the biggest barriers to creating a classroom aesthetic can be the teachers themselves. When many teachers decided to enter the education field, they dreamed of what their classrooms would look like. Some early educators likely dreamed about bright, colorful classrooms with rainbow mobiles hanging from the ceilings. The additional sensory stimulation excites them as opposed to causing them stress. However, it is important for them to remember that not all children can be successful in a brightly colored classroom environment. Although it can be challenging for any adult to change their expectations, teachers want their students to be successful. These teachers will often change their classroom design when they see how it can benefit their students.

The aesthetic classroom aims to bring a reasonable amount of natural characteristics into the indoor classroom. Neurodivergent children can also benefit from increased access to the outdoors. Our next chapter will specifically look at the outdoor classroom.

CHAPTER 5:

The Outdoor Classroom

Today's children spend less time outside each day than any previous generation (National Recreation and Park Association, n.d.). The results of these changes can be seen in increased screen time and a more sedentary lifestyle. Less time outside has also affected the health of children through increased childhood obesity or through mental health changes. One additional change to consider is the effect on a child's education by spending less time outside. Of course, changes to a child's mental and physical health directly affect a child's ability to learn, but it is important to identify that the outdoor environment provides children with a great deal of learning. When the average child only has four to seven minutes of outdoor unstructured play each day, it affects all areas of the child's development (National Recreation and Park Association, n.d.). One way that education specialists have begun to address this concern is by looking at the effect of the outdoor classroom on the physical, mental, emotional, and academic development of young children.

What Is the Outdoor Classroom?

Many individuals have different ideas about what an outdoor classroom is. The outdoor classroom is not simply a playground. It is more structured. The outdoor classroom is a specific outdoor area on the school grounds or in an area of nature close to the school that is designed for classroom learning (OutClass, 2025). It includes seating and space for group activities. It is also close enough to free space that children have the opportunity to observe nature and participate in activities such as nature walks. This type of outdoor classroom can be used for any age group of children.

The outdoor classroom is often confused with forest school. Forest schools emerged in the United Kingdom in 1993 and have now spread throughout the globe (Forest School Association, n.d.; Maynard, 2007). Forest school takes place in the forest or the natural environment. This approach to learning has many of the same types of activities as the outdoor classroom; however, forest school is specifically created to be outdoors. The outdoor classroom is one part of a typical school experience. The students may still use the indoor classroom for part of the school day; however, a teacher who uses the outdoor classroom specifically plans lessons that can be conducted outside and meet the curriculum requirements of the child's age level.

The outdoor classroom focuses on nature integration as part of the education experience (OutClass, 2025). Math, reading, and science activities still take place, but the learning materials include the natural environment. Children have more flexibility in the outdoor classroom to move around, use nontraditional seating, and improvise materials from the natural environment. The learning process is more experiential and hands-on, instead of simply sitting at a desk and having a teacher feed the children information. Many advocates of the outdoor classroom will also state that the outdoor classroom offers more health options for children since there is exposure to vitamin D, fresh air, and additional movement opportunities.

The Benefits of the Outdoor Classroom

Along with the opportunity for increased physical health that comes with being outdoors and being more active, the outdoor classroom has many documented benefits for children.

- **Enhances and develops creativity:** Using the outdoor classroom pulls children away from computer screens and prepackaged learning. Instead, children have to use open-ended learning materials that require them to be innovative in how they solve problems (Pritts, 2024).

- **Increases concentration:** Screens such as laptops and tables have conditioned children to become accustomed to short segments of information (Pritts, 2024). They receive a notification to move on to a new activity, and their attention span resets for the next item. In the outdoor environment, children show increases in their attention with an emphasis on working until completion on projects that they imagined and implemented, instead of ingesting short segments of material.
- **Improves observation skills:** With a live classroom in front of them, children are much more likely to observe what is around them (Pritts, 2024). Some of those observation skills improve through planned activities created by the teacher helping children to look for living creatures, colors, or anomalies in the environment. Other observation habits increase because the outdoor environment is always changing. Unlike the indoor classroom, where materials are found in the same location, the outdoor environment is different every day—movements of insects and other animals, lighting that changes with the time of day and weather, and seasonal changes bring endless variety.
- **Increases student engagement:** Because the outdoor classroom is different from many other educational experiences, and students often get to improvise and create during their lessons, research has shown that students are more engaged in planned lessons in the outdoor classroom (Mann et al., 2022).
- **Encourages better behavior:** Deeper engagement in activities often leads to better behavior in the outdoor classroom (Natural England, 2016). This could be because engagement decreases boredom and the incidence of children finding ways to "entertain" themselves during class. It could also be related to the mental health benefits of increased movement, fresh air, and sunshine.
- **Improves teaching quality:** Teachers seem to be more excited about using the outdoor classroom, just like their students (Natural England, 2016). Teachers reported that they put more energy to planning their lessons and feel that their teaching skills are better when using the outdoor classroom. One possible reason is that teachers are using more creative freedom to develop these lessons instead of prewritten lessons out of standardized textbooks.
- **Improves academic performance:** With increased student engagement and enhanced concentration, it is natural (pun intended!) that students will perform better academically (Williams and Dixon, 2013). Some research shows that students also perform better in the traditional classroom when they have access to an outdoor classroom as well (Bauld, 2021).
- **Improved collaboration and social interaction:** During structured group activities in which students are asked to collaborate with one another, they

have been found to come up with more creative and innovative solutions when using natural materials (Natural England, 2016). These new ideas require students to communicate and work together to make their group projects work.

- **Improved self-confidence:** Students naturally become more confident when their academic performance is improving and they feel that they are successful in school (University College London, 2019). The outdoor classroom allows children who aren't as successful sitting in desks all day to experience success in a new environment. When a student realizes they have the ability to be successful in one educational setting, it often increases their confidence in success in another environment as well.

The Outdoor Classroom and the Neurodivergent Mind

As noted in the previous section, research supports the assertion that typically developing children show benefits in the outdoor classroom (Bauld, 2021). Is it also beneficial for neurodivergent children? There is not as much research specifically on neurodivergent children in the outdoor classroom, but there is a significant amount of information on neurodivergent children benefiting from spending time in an outdoor environment (Li et al., 2019). The benefits of spending time outdoors include:

- Reducing stress
- Enhancing emotional resilience
- Facilitating imaginative play
- Promoting cognitive functioning
- Elevating attention span

Some of the same research studies also indicate that neurodivergent children may have a few barriers to maximizing learning in the outdoor environment (Li et al., 2019). For example, the outdoor classroom can help reduce stress for neurodivergent children, but the amount of sensory stimulation that the children are exposed to and how they handle that stimulation over time can mean that the benefits vary. The outdoor environment has many rich colors, sounds, and textures; sensory-defensive child may find it difficult to spend a great deal of time outdoors with so many stimuli to process. On the other hand, if a child is more accustomed to spending time outdoors, the stimuli may not be as overwhelming. When children first start using an outdoor classroom, there will be a transition process.

Research has shown that neurodivergent children can be successful with more initial adult assistance (Coughlan and Lynch, 2024). In settings where children were just exposed to more outdoor playtime, neurodivergent children didn't necessarily know how to initiate social interactions with peers or participate in group games. Since the outdoor classroom is much more structured than playground time, children naturally get more teacher instruction. Neurodivergent children may need more transitional assistance to become accustomed to using open-ended materials and being able to improvise with their learning assignments. Once that transition occurs and they know what to expect, the outdoor classroom allows for the type of innovation and creativity that many neurodivergent children excel at.

The Outdoor Classroom as a Resource

When schools and teachers have never used an outdoor classroom before, it can be difficult to know where to begin. Teachers can follow these steps to create an outdoor classroom that can benefit students throughout the school.

1. **Get buy-in.** Although a teacher may initially be enthusiastic about teaching outdoors, doing so is a huge concept that needs support from many different people. First, teachers need to approach the school administrator to talk about the reasons the school could benefit from this type of classroom and what type of outcomes the school could see in student progress. This could involve the administrator offering a presentation on the benefits of the classroom, examples of how similar schools have created an outdoor classroom, and cost proposals. Finally, it is also key to get family buy-in. Not only does the school want parents to be excited about a new learning strategy, but the school will probably need parent participation to make the classroom possible.
2. **Get volunteers.** To design, finance, and build an outdoor classroom, the school will need to recruit a large number of volunteers. If the school does not have the money to finance the project out of general funds, then a fundraising committee must be formed. Luckily, an outdoor classroom is not as expensive as an indoor classroom, but funds will be needed to create seating, shade, and some structured learning materials. Finally, when it comes time to build the outdoor classroom, many volunteers will be needed.
3. **Consider the space.** If the school approves the project, the next step is to determine what space will be used so the design team can move forward. The outdoor space may be on the school grounds already, or it may be adjacent to the school in a wooded or other natural environment. When selecting the space, there are several things to consider.

- If it isn't on the school grounds, the space needs to be close in proximity, with a safe walking path for the children.
- It should offer some shade, or the school needs to consider a way to add shade.
- The space should be accessible for all children who will be using it. Many neurodivergent children have issues with balance, muscle tone, or body awareness (Laurie, 2022). This means that surfaces need to be level and clear of major obstructions. Children with low body awareness may need more space between the outdoor materials to avoid bumping into obstacles and falling.

4. **Provide seating for a whole class.** In an outdoor classroom, many schools use tree stumps or logs for the children to sit on, so the seating does not have to be expensive.
5. **Consider storage.** Some type of storage will be needed for learning materials related to the activities. Whatever storage you choose should be weather resistant and secure.
6. **Consider maintenance and upkeep.** Although the major cost of the project will be creating the outdoor classroom, it will need regular upkeep for the students to continue to use it. The school administrators need to determine who is responsible for maintaining the safety and cleanliness of the classroom. It is also essential to determine what funding source will take care of maintenance needs for the classroom; this might not be a school funding source. The school's Parent Teacher Association or another local organization might commit to maintenance and repairs.

Classroom Activities

There is no end to the activities that can be incorporated into the outdoor classroom. The key to these activities is for the teacher to preplan them just like the lesson plans in the traditional classroom. Outdoor activities can incorporate multiple learning domains based on sensory, social-emotional, and academic components.

Neurodivergent children need assistance with balance and motor skills. They need exposure to sensory experiences, but it is more beneficial for them to have exposure to natural light and sounds. They excel at noticing the details in their environment. Based on these needs, here are just a few examples of activities for preschool and elementary school:

- **Mud kitchen:** A mud kitchen is similar to the kitchen in the indoor dramatic play area. It also incorporates a sensory component as children "cook" with mud, sticks, leaves, and acorns. This is making pies at the next level.
- **Nature color hunt:** This activity offers a new level of challenge in observation skills. It is easy to find green and brown in the outdoor classroom, but children may really need to look for details to find reds, pinks, blues, and yellows in their natural environment.
- **Scavenger hunt:** This is another detail-oriented activity that invites children to search for a wide variety of items connected to the learning topic.
- **Bird watching:** This is a great science activity when children are learning about the different kingdoms of animals and all the variations of birds. They can look for birds that are native to their state and region. They can also analyze the color patterns of birds and think about why those colors may be important for the birds.
- **Squirrel activity tally sheets:** As children learn to observe the natural environment, they can document the behavior habits of squirrels or other small animals. Once they have a list of what the animals do in their natural environment, the children can begin to keep a tally sheet of how often they see them do each behavior and judge which behavior is the most common.
- **Nature cupcakes:** This is similar to making mud pies, but the teacher will provide a "recipe" of how much mud and other natural elements are needed to mix together in the batter. Then, children can distribute the batter into a cupcake pan.
- **Sidewalk chalk activities:** Sidewalk chalk can be used outside for a variety of academic activities, such as watering the flower letters. In this activity, the teacher will draw flowers with an alphabet letter inside each one, all over the sidewalk. When the children come outside, the teacher can give them watering cans and ask them to water all the flowers with *A*s or whichever letter they select.
- **Journey stick:** Children will collect nature items on a hike. They will also look for one long stick. When they return from the hike or nature walk, they will glue the nature items onto the large stick as a summary of everything they saw on the walk.
- **Log rolls:** Children can roll down a small hill or on a flat surface. The goal is to improve gross motor movements and sensory processing.
- **Rain art:** This is almost like homemade watercolors. Children draw a chalk picture or paint a picture on thick paper. Then, they can leave the picture outside before a rain to see how the consistency of the picture changes once the rain is added to the picture.
- **Playing in the rain:** All children should have the opportunity to play in the rain. It can help children overcome the fear of storms, and it is great sensory input. Make sure that all children have a dry change of clothes, so they do

not stay wet all day. Also, when children do play in the rain, it should be during a mild rain with no lightning activity or high winds.

- **Dramatic play picnics:** Children can pretend to picnic in the outdoor space. This activity allows for cooperative play as they decide what foods to include, where they will sit, and so on.
- **Leaf rubbings:** Children can learn to identify the differences in leaf types by doing leaf rubbings using paper and chalk or crayons. Then, they can examine the texture differences.
- **Nature alphabet:** This is a fun project for the entire class. They construct an alphabet with parts and pieces of nature. For example, the letter *A* might be composed of sticks and leaves, and the letter *C* may be shaped with a string of acorns.
- **Hopscotch:** This is a good game for developing coordination and balance. The hopscotch board can be drawn with sidewalk chalk or be permanently painted on concrete.
- **Four Square:** This game is similar to playing hopscotch outside, except it adds an element of eye-hand coordination when bouncing a ball.
- **Nature faces:** Just like the full class activity of making a nature alphabet, children can individually make nature faces out of available outdoor materials.
- **Gardening:** Children can plant a small outdoor garden that the class cares for.
- **Farm to table:** Children have the responsibility of a classroom garden, but they also learn about the challenges of growing one's own food and what steps are needed for food to go from the farm to the table.
- **Creating bird feeders:** This activity focuses on following multistep directions, but it can also teach about what local wildlife experiences during season changes. Set up feeders and encourage the children to notice which animals use them and when.
- **Nature journals:** Preliterate children can draw pictures of what they notice. Those who are just learning to form letters can use a combination of letters, drawing, and invented spelling. Once children begin writing words and sentences, they can write about what they observe outdoors each day.
- **Creating and flying kites:** Children can conduct scientific experiments on what makes a kite most successful, then create kites that they can fly in the outdoor classroom.
- **Outdoor theater:** Like an indoor puppet theater, the outdoor classroom can include a small stage for performing. Children can even write their own scripts for performances.

- **Painting rocks:** Children look for and find the best rocks to paint, then paint small pictures on the rocks to be used in classroom rock gardens.

Challenges of the Outdoor Classroom

The outdoor classroom offers many benefits, but to implement it effectively, teachers need to identify and problem-solve potential barriers. Common barriers for the outdoor classroom include family concerns, allergies, space, and structure.

Family Concerns

Some families have concerns about their children spending time outdoors. Usually, those concerns are based on the temperature range or the possibility of a child getting a sunburn. Many child-care programs and schools have rules about what is considered an extreme temperature and when children will not be able to go outside. Also, many state licensing organizations require classrooms to have outdoor time, whether it is structured or unstructured. Explaining the outdoor play and learning policies, as well as the policy on sunscreen, in the parent handbook can help families understand the expectations from the beginning of the school year.

Allergies

It is important for teachers to be aware of children's allergies and how severe those allergies are. The school should have a policy on what teachers and other staff need to do to support a child who has allergies. Children with asthma need access to emergency inhalers when they are outdoors should outdoor pollen and other allergens begin to affect them.

Space

When schools initially begin to plan their outdoor classroom, finding space could be the biggest barrier. If a school is landlocked, they may have to use a smaller space than they initially anticipated. Still, the playground is an essential part of the school. Some schools have purchased small plots of land from neighbors to expand their outdoor classrooms.

Structure

The outdoor classroom should not become an additional playground experience. If teachers become overwhelmed and stop planning structured lessons, then the benefits of the outdoor experience rapidly deteriorate. The reason that this strategy is beneficial for children is that it is still curriculum based, and structured activities are provided. The goal is to see progress on specific outcomes that are based on developmental and academic milestones. To meet those goals, teachers must document activities and assess them for effectiveness. Neurodivergent children will struggle with changes to the outdoor classroom if it is typically used for structured activities then suddenly becomes space for unstructured free time. Understanding classroom expectations and routines is essential for success.

This chapter and the previous two chapters explored how classroom spaces—indoors and out—can support neurodivergent learners. The next four chapters focus on engaging practices and therapeutic strategies that nurture children's development.

CHAPTER 6:

Movement and Dance

I started this book with a story about my son, Robbie. As you may recall from the preface, dance has made a huge difference for Robbie by providing him a unique way to express his emotions, a positive way to demonstrate stim behaviors, and a strategy to participate in group activities.

Dance has not only helped Robbie manage his emotions but also allowed him to thrive both socially and academically. This chapter looks at how educators can use dance and movement to support neurodivergent and neurotypical students alike.

What Is Dance?

Dance is a custom that is recognized in almost every culture. Since the beginning of time, people have taught and demonstrated dance, but what, actually, is dance? To simplify, *dance* is expressive movement. People move their bodies in specific, purposeful ways to express emotions, traditions, and even philosophies. Whether a dancer is trained in a studio or with a tribal elder, or simply develops their own movements, that dancer moves in ways that bring the music and the dance to life and express the dancer's body, mind, and soul. Dances can be learned and practiced over a long period of time, or dancers may use movements that they already know to improvise to music.

Along with the emotional and spiritual implications, dance is also a physical activity that strengthens the body and improves overall fitness. Although dance does not resemble a sport with two opposing teams, it is unique in that it can require group cooperation in the same way that a baseball team or a football team must collaborate. Unlike a team sport, dancers are also able to perform and compete individually. In group dances or in individual dances, a dancer will still work to improve overall physical fitness, including strength, coordination, flexibility, and balance.

Analyzing the components of dance makes it seem like a complicated and challenging art form, yet it is an art that seems to relate so well to children with autism and similar disabilities. For a child who specifically struggles with social and emotional skills, dance can bring a new way for that child to express themselves (Bergman, 2024). At the same time, many neurodivergent children struggle with physical development, including gross motor skills. Dance gives a child the opportunity to grow stronger and work on many of these skills. It also offers an environment that encourages repetition without making the child feel alienated. For children who also have difficulty with sensory processing, dance allows them to feel their bodies move through space and develop the sensory awareness needed to be successful at school and at home. Dance can be introduced in the typical classroom, in the music or physical education classroom, or in a dance studio.

The Benefits of Dance

Dancing can benefit a wide variety of individuals, but it is especially powerful to see that many of the benefits align with the challenges that neurodivergent children and adults experience. Of course, each case of autism is different, as with each neurodivergent diagnosis. Some children specifically struggle more with social and emotional delays, while other children may experience developmental challenges in social and emotional skills, motor skills, and cognitive abilities. Since dance can positively affect each of these developmental domains, it is important to understand the effect that dance can have on an individual with a diagnosed disability, as well as on someone who is typically developing.

Physical Development

At its most basic level, dance is a physical activity. It increases the heart rate and breathing speed to increase the flow of oxygen throughout the body. Repeating this physically intensive activity helps lower blood pressure when the body is resting. When a person dances for longer periods of time (and increases heart and lung function), then the body begins to develop endurance to perform for longer increments of time without overexertion (Dabalsa, 2017). Dancers begin their dance training by repeatedly performing slow and controlled movements, such as a ballet dancer performing pliés at the barre. In the same rehearsal, a dancer may practice jumps and leaps, propelling themselves off the ground with large amounts of exertion. These movements help the dancer to develop strength and muscle tone (Dabalsa, 2017). A dancer often maintains proper posture and keeps their shoulders back while their abdominal muscles are held tightly in place. The core muscles are engaged throughout the time the dancer is working on other controlled movements, so the whole body is developing more muscle control.

Of course, a person walking into a child's ballet class may not see proper posture or refined movement. Initially, young children are simply watching the teacher so they can copy the movements and learn to repeat them. Technique develops over time. As dancers develop stronger muscles, they begin to build the skill to balance in unexpected positions. One of the reasons that many people love to watch professional dancers is to see the unique ways their bodies move. Balance develops at the same time as flexibility and agility. When a dancer becomes aware of their own body in space, they can more easily identify their center of gravity. As they move back and forth, the dancer can move parts of their body to keep the center of gravity stable. The more a dancer moves their body through space, the more they are aware of where their body stops and starts. This is often called the sense of proprioception. Just like we are sensitive to the smells around us and the colors in the room, we also need to develop a sense of how the body is moving and what smaller movements are required to put together strings of large movements. Young children are only just developing their sense of proprioception. They will often run through a room bumping into furniture and knocking others down. They are aware of where they want their body to go, but they are less aware of how their movement affects others in the room. This can easily be seen in a dance recital for young children when one child's uncontrolled movement knocks down a group of students on the stage. The best way for children to develop this sense of body awareness is continually to practice these movements.

In a time when children often sit stationary to watch television or play video games, they need the experience of swinging back and forth on a playground as they soar through space and feel the tips of their toes extending toward the sky. Dance can also give children this type of experience. Leaping through the air and bouncing up and down on the tips of their toes allows children to feel their bodies move and lets them push their physical abilities to their limits. When a skill is not possible at first, the child can practice the technique again and again until it is achievable.

Dancing also has overall physical health benefits that can help every dancer (Dabalsa, 2017). First, many children and adults struggle with establishing a healthy sleep routine. As a cardiovascular activity, dancing can cause a child or an adult to exert themselves to the point of exhaustion. Although that may seem overwhelming, it is good to work hard during the day and be ready to sleep at night. Sleep is when the body and the mind recharge, and without consistent sleep, many children show atypical behavior patterns during the day at school. This can have an effect on academic progress and developing friendships.

Finally, a high level of cardiovascular activity can also help with weight management (Anderson et al., 2024). Too often children and adults are sedentary for long periods during the day. This can lead to the heart not getting the level of exercise it needs to work effectively and can also lead to obesity and type 2 diabetes. Depression is also correlated to weight gain and a lack of exercise. Developing healthy habits early in life can help to combat illness throughout a person's lifespan. When children begin to engage in cardiovascular activities at a young age, they are much more likely to carry those healthy habits into adulthood.

Cognitive Development

Most people see dance as a physical activity, but it also stimulates a great deal of cognitive function—the most complicated portion of dance is that the brain must plan out all these movements (Madhan, 2023). The brain must remember the order and the speed of the movements while recognizing the outside sensory information to make sure the movements occur at the right time. The dancer must hear the music or feel the beat and observe the movements of the other dancers. This sensory information dictates how the brain controls the dancer's progress. So, a dancer who is part of a group must remember the order of the movements, time the movements to the music, and align their own movements to the movements of the other dancers—and problem solve what to do next if the other dancers' movements do not occur as anticipated. This requires a great deal of mental dexterity and forces the dancer's mind to change patterns quickly (Madhan, 2023).

The repetition of dance movements and routines transfers the muscles' movements from the child's short-term memory to their long-term memory. Basic skills become part of complicated patterns that help to develop new neural connections in the brain. Because the child is using cross-body movements to engage both sides of the body and both sides of the brain, that development is enhanced. When new neural connections continue to form, the child's executive function and problem-solving skills develop at a faster pace (Edwards, 2015). Many neurodivergent children (such as those with autism) thrive on patterns and routines. These patterns help to regulate the nervous system when the child feels dysregulated. Other neurodivergent children (such as those with ADHD) may struggle with focus and memory, so repeating the same patterns over and over assists the children with deep memory.

One other significant benefit of dancing is the increase in creativity and imagination. Of course, young dancers start off by simply repeating each movement that they see their dance teacher do. As those movements become part of the dancer's muscle memory, then they can complete one movement after another without consciously thinking about doing so. These rehearsed movements are present in the dancer's mind when they must improvise during a performance or change their movements based on another dancer's performance.

Improvisation in dance may initially emerge out of necessity when a dancer forgets the rehearsed routine and tries to come up with something similar at a moment's notice. Eventually, the dancer can intentionally improvise when they see how certain movements flow into one another naturally or when the tempo or style of the music leads to new movements. Actions that started off as robotic or stiff when the child was a toddler become a tool for creative expression as the child grows older and begins to have higher-level thoughts.

Social and Emotional Development

Although dancers can dance in a group or in a solo performance, many dancers benefit from the social and emotional qualities of learning to dance. Most young dancers begin learning in a group class surrounded by same-age peers. Even for two- and three-year-old children who are simply excited by the idea of wearing a tutu or leaping around the room, learning in a group setting has a lot of benefits. First, the child must learn to follow the directions of the teacher and take turns performing with classmates. Even the simplest of dance classes uses themed music, particular movements, and costumes to tell a story. For young children, they may use the music to tell the plot of a well-known fairy tale, which lays a foundation that dance is a tool to communicate a story.

As children grow older, they begin to identify emotions with the music and the movements of the dance. The music may no longer have words, but the dancer moves their body to match the mood of the music. This is a complex task for a child. The dancer must be able to identify others' emotions (such as what the musician was feeling or expressing in a piece of music), then try to mimic those emotions. When they practice a wide variety of music genres, the dancer must learn to convey a range of emotions. Expressing what they think the emotion looks like allows them to identify their own emotions more easily and those of the people around them.

Group dances allow the individual dancer to express himself, but they also allow the group to express themselves as a whole. One of the first things that an audience member notices when watching a group dance together is whether they are in sync. This can be a difficult skill, particularly for young children. It goes against the dancer's desire to stand out and puts the needs of the group before the needs of the individual. Dancers must learn that syncing movements increases the quality of the performance. This increased level of cooperation can benefit the child in many different areas of development.

Dance also provides emotional benefits that focus on the individual child. First, physical activity of this level naturally produces serotonin, known as the feel-good hormone (Edwards, 2015). The increase of serotonin in the body's system increases happiness, helps the dancer feel calm, increases focus, and helps the dancer to be more emotionally stable. Serotonin and dopamine released while dancing also reduce stress and anxiety (Edwards, 2015). Of course, this can depend on how the dancer views their progress on certain skills. If the dancer uses dancing to express themselves and enjoys using their time that way, then stress and anxiety levels will lower. When the dancer sets goals for learning new skills and accomplishes those goals, that success can lead to increased levels of self-esteem and confidence (Edwards, 2015).

For Robbie, dance elevated his mood, even when he was tired or had a difficult day at school. I could see how much the exercise helped him lift his spirits. I also saw how much he began to identify with the emotional themes of the songs. He wasn't able to identify his own emotions to me when he became overwhelmed, but he was able to identify the emotions of a song. This was a huge step for him. He could tell me when the song was sad and that he needed to act sad. Knowing how to act sad was one of the first steps for him before he could identify when he was sad and state that to me.

Dancing and the Neurodivergent Mind

When we think about children diagnosed with autism and similar neurodivergent conditions, consistent symptoms frequently emerge:

- Reduced ability with social skills and communication
- Sensitivity to environmental changes
- Echolalia (the act of repeating words or phrases someone says)
- Repetitive or recurrent behaviors
- Difficulty showing empathy
- Cognitive delays
- Motor delays
- Difficulty learning through traditional methods
- Obsessive thoughts and behaviors (Resnick, 2023)

When you look at the list of symptoms, many of children's difficulties and needs align with the benefits that dance can offer. For example, neurodivergent children often repeat behaviors. This can be because the repetitive behavior allows the child to learn, or it can also be that a familiar behavior can help to soothe the child when they are experiencing increased stress levels. The repetitive behaviors can even be related to an obsession. We often see the media focus on this trait of autism when a young child is intensely focused on trains, dinosaurs, or another field in which the child learns in-depth knowledge. Because dance requires practice and repetition of specific moves, it gives a neurodivergent child a positive outlet for their repetitive behaviors. Instead of being considered obsessive, the child can be viewed as diligent at learning a new skill. The repetitive movement can also be soothing and support the child's sensory processing needs.

Motor Skill Development

Neurodivergent children who struggle with motor skills can master individual skills through repetition and can develop stronger muscle tone. Many children with large muscle delays struggle with coordination and balance; these are some of the basic skills that dance develops. Even for children who do not dance frequently, practicing balancing on one foot or using deep squats helps to develop core muscles that support whole-body coordination. Developing core muscles in the abdomen is critical for children to be able to sit with good posture and eventually develop legible handwriting.

Cognitive Skills Development

Children with cognitive development delays may struggle with following multistep directions or with executive function that controls planning, self-control, or decision-making. This type of learning process is embedded in training for dance. Dancers begin by learning one dance skill at a time, such as a single foot position or arm position. As children master individual skills, instructors show them how to put those skills together in combinations. The dancer may complete a combination one time during the course of a dance, or the combination may be part of a repeating pattern.

As the young dancer works to memorize the steps for an entire dance, they are stringing together many different steps and memorizing the order of each body position. Should the dancer make a mistake, they must learn how to correct it and move back into the correct pattern. This skill set includes motor planning, memorization, long-term memory, and problem-solving skills, and all can be accomplished in a short, two- or three-minute dance taught to preschool-age students. After students have been dancing for three or four years, these movement combinations no longer take as much effort for the brain to plan, and the dancer is able to rely on muscle memory to complete the actions. Many neurodivergent children struggle with motor planning and initially planning a sequence of actions. Dance establishes motor planning to help children learn to plan out their actions and follow through step by step, even when they are feeling dysregulated or are having a hard time connecting to their bodies' movements.

Social and Emotional Development

Neurodivergent children often have difficulty with identifying and expressing their emotions. Some neurodivergent children are nonverbal, but others may have a huge vocabulary and struggle to find the correct words to express themselves. Dance allows these children to express emotions in a physical form instead. Children can select loud and punctuated music to express feelings of anger or slow and mournful music to express sadness. They can change the speed and the fluidity of their movements to accentuate emotions regardless of their ability to articulate their feelings verbally.

The same children who struggle to express their emotions may also find it challenging to interact with their peers. Dancing can place children in purposeful interactions with children their own age so they can learn how to cooperate. Once children have had an opportunity to interact with one another in a setting with adult instruction, they can begin to imitate those interactions in less structured settings and simply learn how to talk and have fun with one another.

Dance as a Resource

There are many ways for a young child to begin participating in dance. Many preschool and elementary school teachers use some form of dance in the classroom several times a week. Some teachers may begin by using instructional music by singers such as Greg and Steve, Dr. Jean, or Raffi, who play music while instructing children how to move. Songs such as "The Freeze" by Greg and Steve simply give children the opportunity to move their bodies however they want, until the music pauses and they are instructed to freeze. Other songs may instruct children to use their bodies to make certain shapes or to move in different ways such as skipping and galloping. For teachers with no background in dance, this is an excellent place to start introducing dance concepts, since the children still get to feel their bodies move through space and some motor planning is required. Also, the children often participate during a group gathering or circle time, so they can work together and enjoy each other's company.

As schools look at new and inventive ways to include the arts in their curriculum, teachers are finding ways to expose more children to dance education. Many early childhood programs have found ways to bring specialized dance teachers to their students. The two most common methods of including dance education are offering a mobile program that visits the center one or two days a week, allowing interested families to enroll their children in an optional dance class, or having all children participate with enrollment fees included in the program tuition.

Program administrators may choose to allow families to opt in or out of participation based on paying an additional enrollment fee; however, doing so may prevent many children who could excel at dance from participating. This is particularly true for little boys, whose families might see dance class as an activity strictly meant for little girls. When the program is offered to every child in an age group (including children with disabilities), then children may benefit from dance in ways that their families did not expect.

Bringing in a specialty teacher also allows the general classroom teachers to observe and learn new skills that may be beneficial for the regular classroom curriculum. This can be especially true on rainy days when children cannot play outdoors and the teachers must plan some type of large muscle activities to help the children release some energy.

As children move into elementary school, we see that both music teachers and physical education teachers plan units on dance to meet the statewide curriculum requirements. This can include units on a variety of styles, including square dancing, ballet, or hip-hop dance. The general goals for the unit may be different depending on which specialty teacher is offering the instruction. Physical education teachers may focus on the physical health benefits of dance, as well as coordinated movements. Music teachers may focus on children moving to the beat of the music and using dance to express a story or emotion. In some elementary schools, the music teacher and the physical education teacher will partner to teach the dance units so the children can get the content multiple times per week—and so specific instruction can be given if the children need help learning the foot and arm formations. For children with motor delays, the special education teacher may also assist in dance classes to help a student with disabilities participate in the same class as peers of similar ages.

In some elementary schools, where the dance curriculum has been successful in the music and physical education classrooms, teachers have also started after-school extracurricular activities where students can spend more time learning dance and having occasional opportunities to perform at school and for their families. Since there are so many genres of dance, these school clubs can look very different depending on the school. Schools may introduce dance troupes that learn a variety of dance styles, or they may focus on specific types of dance such as step dance, ballet, or international dances. Some schools incorporate a music component, such as a drumming and dance club, to expand on the musical curriculum as well.

Gifted-and-talented programs have begun to look beyond simply identifying children based on reading and math scores and are identifying children who are gifted in the arts. Depending on a school system's resources, children may be identified as gifted in visual art, music, or dance beginning as young as elementary school. In some school districts, this means that a teacher at the school nominates the child to be part of the gifted and talented program, and a specialty teacher (such as a dance instructor) may visit the child several times per month and pull the student out of their classroom for advanced instruction. If a child is identified as gifted in dance, the teacher may come to the school and spend an hour with a group of students teaching simple steps, eventually teaching the students to put those steps together in a combination that looks like a short dance. Over several months, the teacher may help the children choreograph an entire dance that is performed at a school event.

Other schools have looked at ways to immerse children in the arts daily, such as magnet schools for creative and performing arts. In a magnet program, the children would receive all the traditional curriculum for each grade level, along with additional arts education incorporated each day. Of course, when there are no options for dance during the school day, the teacher can still be a resource for the family that is trying to find ways to support a neurodivergent child. Many families automatically think of finding an occupational therapist or a counselor to support a child with a disability, but the classroom teacher can offer suggestions of other resources that might assist the child in different ways. It is helpful for a teacher to explain to family members why a weekly dance class could benefit a child who is attempting to overcome so many obstacles. When the school does not provide these types of nontraditional learning environments, it can be important for teachers to keep an up-to-date resources list to advise families.

Teachers should be aware of several things before recommending dance classes to families with neurodivergent children. First, does the dance studio have a philosophy about working with children with special needs, and are staff members trained on different types of disabilities? Second, what are the typical class sizes like? Would a child get the individual attention needed, or would they be overwhelmed by the excitement and size of the class? Finally, if the dance studio does not have experience working with children with disabilities, would they be open to learning and making accommodations? It could also be helpful to know general information about the cost in case it is too expensive for many families to afford.

Classroom Activities

When you consider the motor development of young children, each age group has different skills to focus on when you introduce dance activities into the general classroom. Toddlers and young preschoolers (between the ages of one and three years) are developing muscle coordination and balance control (Krasnow and Wilmerding, 2021). Older preschoolers and kindergarten students will have more erratic muscle responses and more variability with their sensory integration, so they need to work on balance and strength. Elementary school–aged students will have mastered more control of their bodies and can mimic the movements of adults, but they have slower response times than full-grown adults.

Based on these traits, teachers need to plan activities that will help each age group move to the next set of developmental skills. Activities for toddlers and preschoolers should focus on early locomotor skills, but these skills need to be introduced in a play-based way to engage the children and help the learning process. Early locomotor skills include the following:

- **Jumping:** Around the age of two, a child should be able to jump with both feet in a symmetrical movement. Teachers can incorporate activities where children jump like frogs, jump over small block buildings, or play hopscotch on the playground.
- **Galloping:** Between the ages of two and three, a child should begin galloping with asymmetrical movement but with the same foot consistently in the lead.
- **Hopping:** This skill requires a child to have both strength and balance because the child must remain stable on one foot. Because hopping can remain on the same foot, it is not the most complicated of the early locomotor activities.
- **Skipping:** Skipping is more complicated than hopping because alternating the legs requires more coordination. Only 20 percent of four-year-olds can skip correctly (Krasnow and Wilmerding, 2021).

As young children enter early elementary school, they can practice more complicated locomotor activities. Children should be challenged to balance even when their eyes are closed. They can begin to improvise their movements based on the speed and genre of music that is playing. They can also begin to dance and move as part of team activities.

Beginning with preschool students and moving up to early elementary students, classroom teachers can practice some of the following activities to help students develop the balance and coordination, which eventually will be needed to master dance techniques:

- **Freeze Dance:** The popular children's musicians Greg and Steve (https://www.gregandsteve.com) have a wonderful song called "The Freeze." It is an instructional dance that tells children to move their bodies to the music until they hear the music pause, then the children must freeze in place. Teachers can do the same activity with a piece of instrumental music and simply pause the music when the children must freeze (stop moving). Using new music each time will require the children to listen more closely because they don't know at what point the music will stop and restart.

- **Interactive songs:** Preschool teachers have been using interactive songs for decades, such as "The Hokey Pokey," "Head, Shoulders, Knees, and Toes," "The Chicken Dance," and "The Cha Cha Slide." These songs help the dancer learn to move their body with purpose, since the songs give specific instructions on how to move. The dancer must move to the words and to the tempo of the music.
- **Dance like an animal:** This activity allows the dancer to explore creative movement. It is the first step toward improvisation; however, the dancer has some idea of how to move their body since the animal has distinct characteristics. Children often begin learning about animals as soon as they can talk and move, so this activity is culturally relevant for dancers from a variety of backgrounds. It also allows children to think about body part awareness, which will be essential for the dancers as they grow and develop, because they must identify how the animal travels and what parts of the body are used in each movement.
- **Change the beat:** For this type of activity, the teacher would need to have a collection of music with different tempos and rhythms, as well as different genres of music. Children would need to use their musicality skills to move their bodies to the speed and articulation of the music. When the teacher changes the type of music, the dancer would compare and contrast the two musical pieces in their head and decide how to change their body movements to match the music. This activity can also expose young dancers to a wide variety of cultural experiences, depending on the variety of music that the teacher assembles. It is also a great opportunity to involve families and ask them to send in music selections from different cultural backgrounds.
- **Prop dancing:** Prop dancing can include rhythm sticks, scarves, egg shakers, or other items that relate to the theme of the music. Instrumental props can be used to emphasize the musicality of the dance piece, such as tapping out the beat as students move to the music. Props such as scarves move through space at their own speed, so dancers learn the difference between moving their bodies and moving the props. Props can be the focus of the dance, or the dancer can simply use the item as an accent during the dance. Props allow for creative movement, but there is a strong emphasis on locomotor movement because additional coordination may be required to dance with the items in hand.

Challenges to Dance Education

Children may encounter obstacles that can limit their access to dance education. One of the most common is the gender bias associated with dance. Unlike music and visual arts training, many people view dance as a feminine art form, so families may prefer that young boys not participate. This seems to be slightly less of a problem in preschool, but as boys enter elementary school, many families may not feel that boys can be dancers. It is important for children to see all different types of dancers and all different styles of dance to combat some of these stereotypes. Many cultural dance customs value men and women dancing in their ceremonies. Ballet may be seen as more feminine compared to other styles of dance, but children benefit from seeing male and female ballet dancers and learning what their roles are in the dance. Field trips and occasions when visiting performers come to schools are key opportunities to educate children about these variations. It is also important for teachers to provide books and pictures that show dancers of different genders and different ethnicities, since the media may portray that some styles of dance are only associated with one ethnic background.

Another challenge to introducing dance to young students can be finding trained instructors. Many teachers feel comfortable leading art projects, but they do not feel knowledgeable enough to teach children a pattern of dance steps. Teachers can learn along with their students. Preschool-age students are not learning complicated dance sequences. They can start by trying to move their bodies in a way that matches the music. Children can identify the emotions of music and how the music makes them feel.

One challenge that may particularly affect neurodivergent children is overcoming the social anxiety component of dance (Montaser et al., 2023). Even preschool-aged students can begin experiencing some level of social anxiety. Children begin to wonder if their peers are watching and judging them. This type of social anxiety is common for neurodivergent children, since they struggle so much with social interactions. When these children first begin dancing in a group setting, they may be reserved because they wonder if their peers are watching them and if they look "silly" while dancing. This anxiety can be diminished when the teacher gives children examples of how to move and participates in the classroom activities as a model. More insecure children can mirror the adult instead of anxiously worrying about what to do next.

It is also important for teachers to remember to use community and parent resources. Parent volunteers may be willing to come to school and offer dance instruction to the children while instructing the teacher at the same time. At the elementary-school level, an after-school club can be led by a teacher or community volunteer. Even community resources such as the public library or the parks and recreation department may be able to provide instruction or volunteers who can help establish dance education. Once an initial curriculum is established, the classroom teacher may be able to move forward with only occasional assistance.

Dance offers children the ability to move their bodies to regulate their nervous system and their emotions; however, it is not the only method of self-regulation. The next chapter will focus on how to begin teaching young children calming techniques so they have the ability to self-regulate whenever necessary.

CHAPTER 7:
Mindfulness and Calming Practices

The previous chapter describes how dance and movement can support both neurodivergent and neurotypical children. Along those same lines, mindfulness practices can greatly benefit neurodivergent children, their neurotypical peers, and the teachers and other adults in the classroom. Everyone gains from a calm and inviting classroom environment.

What Is Mindfulness?

Mindfulness is being aware of both your inner emotional state and your surroundings, including the people around you and the environment (American Psychological Association, 2025). For children, mindfulness focuses on what the child needs to calm down (Garey, 2024b). That often includes slowing down the body, focusing on breathing, and becoming aware of current emotions. Since many children are still learning how to identify their emotions under the best of circumstances, it can be a struggle to be mindful amid daily chaos.

To achieve mindfulness and a state of calm, children need to learn to manage stress, identify their emotions, and cope with unexpected situations that come up in daily life. This type of mindfulness is not associated with religion, although many religions talk about peace or a state of calm. Instead, this type of mindfulness is associated with self-regulation, which can be a huge challenge for neurodivergent children.

The goal for teachers is to teach children to pay attention to their thoughts and emotions so they can control their bodies and manage impulse control. It is almost impossible to teach children to manage their emotions during a meltdown. At that point, the child is not rational, and they simply need time to work their emotions out. Instead, the goal is to teach children these self-regulation skills when they are in a calm and nurturing environment. The children need to become so comfortable with these calming activities that when they are exposed to intense stress, they can identify their emotions and fall back on calming techniques that are already second nature.

Mindfulness includes skills that are often categorized as executive function skills, the most complex skills that the brain can master (Calderon, 2020). These skills include impulse control, working memory, and cognitive flexibility (or the ability to transition and problem solve). These skills don't develop in a linear progression, and the part of the brain responsible for executive function does not fully develop until the early twenties. However, these skills do initially begin to develop in early childhood, so it is important to begin guiding children to use them at a young age.

Many different environmental factors can affect a child's ability to use executive functioning skills, including stress levels, adverse childhood experiences, the child's home life, and the child's educational opportunities (Calderon, 2020). Many more young children seem to be experiencing chronic stress and anxiety, and these factors can have a major effect on a child's ability to self-regulate and calm their own mind and body.

Research has shown that mindfulness and calming practices directly affect the brain (Linder, 2019). Different portions of the brain are affected in different ways:

- **Prefrontal cortex:** Mindfulness and calming practices increase the activity in the prefrontal cortex, which is responsible for executive functioning as well as rational thought, intentional planning, and impulse control (Rathore et al., 2023).
- **Amygdala:** The amygdala is responsible for some of the brain's most basic fight-or-flight responses, as well as trauma symptoms. Mindfulness and calming processes are highly correlated with a decrease in the amygdala's activity.
- **Social neural connectivity:** Mindfulness and calming practices show links in the parts of the brain that establish relationships and maintain those relationships over time.

- **Anterior cingulate cortex:** This portion of the brain focuses on motivation, the ability to focus, and motor control. Mindfulness and calming practices show high correlations to activity in this portion of the brain and increasing uninterrupted cognitive attention.
- **Insula:** The insula is the body's center for interoception, the sense of body awareness that alerts the brain to concepts such as hunger, thirst, muscle tension, and so on. Many people also relate the insula to the center of "gut" instincts. When individuals practice mindfulness and calming practices, they are better able to identify interoception needs, since mindfulness focuses on body awareness.

The Benefits of Mindfulness and Calming Practices

Mindfulness activities can support children's ability to learn emotional balance and stress management. Other benefits of mindfulness practices may include the following:

- Children can focus more despite outside distractions.
- Children can identify their own emotions and the emotions of others.
- Children can express their emotions to others once they know how they feel.
- Children can control their emotions during transitions or stressful situations.
- Children can be patient instead of relying on immediate gratification.
- Children can increase their impulse control skills.
- Children can communicate (verbally or nonverbally) during stressful situations.
- Children can demonstrate problem-solving skills when they are not strictly focused on the stress of the moment.
- Children can have successful friendships when they can identify their own emotions and the emotions of a peer (Wedge, 2018).

The combination of all these developing skills leads to a better sense of well-being for the child and more self-confidence.

Mindfulness and the Neurodivergent Mind

Many neurodivergent children struggle with social communication and differences in the neurological system compared to neurotypical children. They can experience challenges related to coping with changes in routines, identifying their emotions and physical needs, and coping with high stress levels (Ridderinkhof, de Bruin, Blom, and Bögels, 2017). These relate to skills that mindfulness can directly affect. Many neurodivergent children have extensive therapy to support their social-emotional growth and de-escalate their response to stressors in their environment. Executive function skills could be improved by helping children to reflect on experiences, focus attention for longer periods of time, and slow down impulse control reactions.

Mindfulness practices could also improve a child's social and communication skills. The initial steps for social and emotional skill development are to identify the components of the child's own emotions and begin to identify when they are feeling angry, stressed, or sad. Once the child begins to identify their own emotions, they can begin to understand the emotions of others, including recognizing facial expressions and actions that may indicate how individuals are feeling. Mindfulness activities can help to establish this level of emotional intelligence and build on it, so the child can communicate with others about their feelings or what they perceive are the feelings of others.

Another key aspect of mindfulness practices that can support neurodivergent children is a focus on coping skills (Ridderinkhof, de Bruin, Blom, and Bögels, 2017). Coping skills are complex and can involve a variety of skills, including developing focus, increasing impulse control, problem solving, identifying emotions, and finding a way to self-regulate in the midst of anger or disappointment. Many of these skills are more executive functions of the brain; however, they also build upon foundational social and emotional skills that are all a part of mindfulness practices.

Raising a neurodivergent child can be stressful. Families could also benefit from learning and practicing these mindfulness practices, both to increase their own mindfulness and calming skills and to guide children toward using these skills when they are overwhelmed and emotional. Disciplining and instructing a neurodivergent child requires families to maintain calm and be intentional with their emotions and their instructions (Arky, 2025). Parents set an example of emotional regulation for children who are trying to learn these skills (Buss, 2024). Because their own self-regulation is so important, parents of neurodivergent children can help their own children by demonstrating these behaviors.

Calming Practices as a Resource

Although teachers can implement specific activities that can teach skills for calming, it is also important to implement practices for mindfulness in the classroom as a whole. These practices can guide the children through various group and individual activities, enhancing their coping and problem-solving skills. For teachers to see the benefits, they must implement mindfulness and calming at the full classroom level, as well as individual activities.

When implementing mindfulness practices, teachers should consider targeted implementation for the times in the school day that are the most chaotic: arrival, dismissal, transitions, and so on. These are the times when children can benefit the most from calming practices. Teachers need to pick strategies to implement during these times of day that can benefit the class as a whole and make a conscious effort to help students learn the skills they need.

A classroom is composed of so many different students, and some of them may have conflicting needs. For example, some might seek sensory stimuli, and others might be defensive to sensory-rich situations. It is hard to find strategies that support every child, but it is important to think of the children who need targeted supports and to consider multiple IEP goals. Which techniques will work for the majority of the classroom without causing a major conflict for other students? When a teacher decides to implement a mindfulness technique, it may not be successful immediately. The teacher needs to model the behavior and allow the children time to practice the skill. After children feel comfortable, the teacher can begin to assess whether the strategy is working or if accommodations need to be made. When a teacher is attempting to establish a calm classroom environment, they need to establish some foundational skills before looking for more specific strategies.

Consistent Daily Routine

As discussed in chapter 3, the classroom must have a consistent routine so children know what to expect each day. When children can anticipate what comes next in the school day, they are less likely to be stressed. For older students, this does not mean that the schedule needs to be the same each day; they simply need to understand what the routine and expectations are.

Quiet Area

The classroom should be set up so a child can have alone time if needed. One way that students learn to calm themselves is by having a moment of privacy. In elementary school, a student may just need to go to the restroom or to visit the special education classroom to find temporary solitude. Preschool students need an option for alone time within the classroom, such as a tent or a quiet area that allows for solitude. (Note: The quiet area should not be used as a disciplinary consequence.) Explain these opportunities at the beginning of the school year, so children can self-regulate and find solitude without bothering other students.

Personal Space

Whenever possible, the classroom design should ensure that students have enough personal space without classmates bumping up against them. A lack of personal space can be a stressor for many students. If children sit at tables for group work, they should have enough space to complete work without directly touching another child.

Quiet Work Time

It is also important for teachers to establish daily time in the schedule for independent work, with the expectation of a quieter atmosphere in the classroom. Not all students can handle continuous noise and activity well, and if they don't get a calmer, quieter environment at some point during the day, it can lead to emotional outbursts.

Emotional Expression

Finally, it is important for teachers to establish a classroom environment where students can talk about their feelings. It is also crucial for students to be able to cry in class without feeling ashamed. Some students do not have a home life that encourages emotional expression, so they may initially tell peers to stop crying or to control their emotions; however, expressing emotions freely can become part of the classroom culture if the teacher reinforces the strategy.

Classroom Activities

Many different activities can help children slow down the speed of their bodies and be more aware of what is going on around them. Blowing bubbles is a great example. Most children already have had the experience of blowing bubbles. In most cases, that means when a child blows bubbles, they will try to produce as many bubbles as possible and run around trying to pop each bubble before anyone else can. To use bubbles as a calming activity and to get the children to slow down their breathing, the teacher can encourage them to blow the largest bubble possible without letting it pop. The teacher should present the activity when the children are already listening and then demonstrate it. Bubbles are fragile, so the children will have to slow down their breathing and use a more sustained stream of air. When the bubbles do pop, the teacher can calmly encourage the children to try again with slower, steadier breaths.

Some mindfulness activities can be a tool for the whole class to experience at one time, but others can be used for individual children. Regardless of the style of the activity, it is still necessary for the teacher to demonstrate the activity to the children in a large or small group setting, so every child in the class understands how to use the activity. Then, when a child wants to use the material individually, they know how and can practice mindfulness independently.

Classroom Nature Walks

Taking children out to walk in nature can enhance overall body awareness, increase deep breathing, and increase the movement that many children need for self-regulation. When the teacher is walking with the children, it is a great time to ask them about the smells, sounds, and colors that are all around them. Teachers can also ask children to collect "souvenirs" from their walk, such as leaves, stones, and flowers, that connect children to the natural environment.

Yoga

Using yoga in the classroom increases strength and increases body awareness. Many children already have a great deal of body flexibility, so it may be easier for the children to participate than it is for the teacher. If the whole class participates in yoga together, they need enough space for every child to stretch out and participate fully. The teacher may offer group yoga and allow the children to take turns participating. Yoga can also be an individual activity; set out a yoga mat and picture cards of different poses that the children can model. Children often feel more invested when the yoga picture cards feature their classmates doing the poses.

The children may be invited to bring a "yoga buddy"—a stuffed doll or an action figure from home—to participate in yoga positions in a group or individually with the child. The child would first pose the buddy into the yoga position, such as Downward Facing Dog. This would help the child grasp how the body should be shaped for the pose. After posing the buddy, the child would imitate the position.

Rain Stick Calming

As an individual activity, a rain stick can be a calming addition to a quiet corner of the classroom. The child can turn the rain stick back and forth and quietly listen to the sound. The teacher should demonstrate how to use the rain stick before setting it out for use. During the demonstration, the teacher can ask the children questions about what they hear when the rain stick turns, what the sound reminds the children of, and what places they think of when they hear the sound. This could also be a calming activity that is available to children when they become overwhelmed and need to self-regulate. To allow the children to use the rain stick whenever they feel emotionally overwhelmed, it should be accessible throughout the day and not just during free-choice time.

Calm Down Jars

Calm down jars (or sensory jars) are easy to make. They can contain a variety of items such as water, glitter, food coloring, and oil (baby oil or cooking oil). Depending on the theme of the bottle, you could add items such as seashells, beads, or small plastic toys to plastic jars or bottles. Then, hot-glue the top onto the jar on so a child can't easily take the top off. A child can shake the bottle with all their strength, then watch as all the items inside slowly settle. This activity allows children to use energetic and aggressive movements, as well as slow and calming movements.

Classroom Fish Tanks

There is a reason that so many hospitals and doctors' offices have fish tanks. It is easy to lose track of time by watching fish gracefully move through the water. When the tank has a variety of different fish, children can compare the speed of the fish as they move back and forth. Brightly colored fish allow children to process different sensory stimulation.

Blowing on Pinwheels

Similar to blowing bubbles, blowing on a pinwheel can help a child with maintaining slow, steady breathing. Also, depending on what the pinwheel looks like (shiny, attractive colors), it can cause the child to focus intently on the pinwheel for an extended period of time.

Playing with Clay

Playing with clay is a multisensory experience. Since clay is so dense, it requires a lot of strength and focus for a child to manipulate it and create shapes. The tactile experience can help children who need additional sensory input. Also, it can allow children the repetitive movements they need to self-regulate and relax.

Bear Hugs

Sometimes, children just need to feel deep pressure. Depending on the child's preference, they may need to give or receive a bear hug.

Breathing with Shapes

In this activity, the teacher would provide large construction paper shapes for all the children in the group. They slowly trace the outside of the shape as they inhale, then trace the shape again while exhaling. This helps the children regulate the speed of breathing.

Feelings Charades

After the teacher explains the game of charades, the children can each act out an emotion without using any words. Then, the rest of the class or a small group can guess which emotion the child selected. In this activity, the teacher may need to take the first turn and demonstrate how to act out an emotion.

Playing with Puppets

Puppets give children the opportunity to act out their feelings when they may not have the skill set to identify the emotions they are feeling at a particular moment. They can also act out situations that have occurred in their own life again and again until they can emotionally process them.

Feather Balance

The teacher can give each child a feather and challenge them to balance it on a hand, an elbow, or on their nose. This activity requires the child to slow down their body, slow their breathing, and concentrate on overall body awareness.

Scarf Dancing

The teacher passes out individual scarves to each child who is participating, then selects music that allows children to move their scarves to the speed and rhythm of the music. It is important for teachers to participate in scarf dancing to demonstrate potential movements for children who may not initially understand what the teacher is asking them to do. Depending on the range of music (preferably instrumental) that the teacher selects, students may demonstrate a wide range of movements and energy levels during the activity.

Wall Push-Ups

Children who have a lot of energy may benefit from wall push-ups. This activity requires the child to focus their energy and use precise movements. It also helps children who may need deep pressure to self-regulate.

Rocking in a Rocking Chair

Every classroom can benefit from having a child-sized rocking chair. The movement can improve coordination and balance as children move back and forth. It also can benefit children who need stim behavior to self-regulate. Children can adjust the speed at which they move back and forth as their moods allow. Rocking can also be a relaxing experience.

Popping Bubble Wrap

Everyone loves bubble wrap! Children love to pop every single bubble, so this activity lets them focus on popping bubbles and block out the rest of the world. Plus, there is something very rewarding about knowing that you accomplished a task and burst every bubble on your piece of bubble wrap. The only challenge is keeping bubble wrap in the classroom for more than one day.

Painting to Music

Painting to music can be an individual activity or done in a group. Again, the teacher will probably want to select an instrumental playlist that has a variety of songs with different tempos and a range of fluidity (for example, choppy/staccato or smooth/legato). In a small group, the teacher would set up the activity for each child to have paper, paint, and a paintbrush. When the music begins, the children can paint what they hear. If the child participates in the activity individually, then headphones can be set up in the art area next to the easel. The child can wear the headphones with the instructions to "paint like the music."

Having a Dance Party

Sometimes, the whole class just needs to dance it out! A dance party with raucous music allows children to move their bodies in a variety of positions, move to the music, and express themselves.

Just Yelling!

When a child has pent-up emotions, it can be beneficial to have the opportunity to yell. If a child does need to yell, then the teacher will need set up a situation so other children in the classroom are not overwhelmed with sensory information. For example, the teacher might walk the child outside, away from the building, and tell them that this is a chance to scream until they can't scream anymore. The emotional release of screaming can be centering, and it also reassures the child that it is okay to be upset. Screaming has to occur in an appropriate place; then the child can return to the classroom.

Challenges of Mindfulness and Calming Practices

A classroom of twenty to thirty young children is naturally chaotic, so implementing calming techniques is challenging. The best way for teachers to be successful is to be consistent in the approach. Mindfulness must be a daily part of the classroom to make it a foundation of the classroom. Along with inconsistency, there are other obstacles that a teacher can encounter when setting up a mindful classroom.

Families and caregivers may not understand the importance of mindfulness and may have concerns over why the teacher is spending time setting up this type of learning environment. Some parents may feel that a mindfulness philosophy is related to some type of religious principle that conflicts with the one the family currently practices. Most of this concern can be addressed by educating parents on what type of mindfulness activities are used in the classroom and how they benefit the children in the class. Once parents understand that their children are reaping the benefits of a certain teaching style, they are often more open-minded. Sometimes, changing the vocabulary, such as using "calming practices" instead of *mindfulness*, can help families better understand the overall intent of the teaching strategies and help them to be more supportive.

As we continue to look at effective classroom practices for neurodivergent classrooms, we will now move on to a slightly more concrete strategy by looking at art and music as a therapy tool.

CHAPTER 8:

Art and Music Therapy

For years, teachers have been using art and music to help children learn to control their bodies and express their emotions. The reality of expressive art forms is that the artists themselves may have created their compositions and portraits for the same reasons.

What Are Art and Music Therapy?

Art and music therapy are forms of therapy conducted by a certified mental health specialist who uses art or music as a way to support children so they can learn coping skills, become more self-aware and self-confident, reduce stress, and even become aware of feelings and emotions that they have not been able to process yet (American Art Therapy Association, 2022). Artists and musicians focus on using their skills to create a final product or performance; art and music therapy focus more on the process of creating art and music to support children's development. Therapy goals align with many of the typical goals of the early childhood classroom, where teachers focus on teaching the process of the creative arts instead of the final product.

Of course, early education teachers are not therapists and should not attempt to assume that role. Yet, even without a therapist's certification, teachers in the preschool or elementary school classroom can employ methods used by an art or music therapist that can be helpful for students, especially those who are neurodivergent. Additionally, the school guidance counselor can use some of these techniques when working with neurodivergent students in a one-on-one setting.

The Benefits of Art and Music on Child Development

Researchers have extensively studied the benefits of art and music to the developing mind of the young child. Children who are exposed to the arts at a young age, predominantly before the age of seven, have a slightly different brain structure than those who have not had that exposure (UPMC Health Beat, 2014). Learning music and art can increase the grey matter of the brain, which helps with processing and retrieving information. An increased number of neural connections also indicates increased brain volume (Center on the Developing Child, 2025). These increased brain connections help with intellectual and social-skills development such as reading comprehension, mathematics, short- and long-term memory development, and even motor skills.

Research shows that when music and art are used as therapeutic tools, they can help with expressing emotions, reducing anxiety, improving focus, and growing communication skills, whether verbal or nonverbal (Johns Hopkins Medicine, 2025). Neither art therapy nor music therapy requires any specific level of skill from the patients. The main goals include self-realization and expression, so whatever skill set the patient has would be sufficient.

Art and Music Therapy and the Neurodivergent Mind

Art and music therapy have become popular treatments for neurodivergent children and adults. When working with a neurodivergent child, the primary goals for art and music therapy include the following:

- Increasing communication skills and expression

- Improving social skills and establishing relationships
- Overcoming sensory challenges (Zauderer, 2023)

Because each neurodivergent child is going to have different needs based on their individual diagnosis, the therapy will focus on the goals that are appropriate for the individual. Music therapists may focus on using rhythm activities, singing songs, and playing instruments (AdinaABA, 2024). Art therapists may use a variety of art media such as paint, clay, collage, and simple drawing (Zauderer, 2023). Since both methods of therapy include a variety of sensory stimuli, the therapists may slowly integrate new sensory experiences and eventually hope to desensitize the child to some of their sensory-defensive behaviors. Research has shown that when neurodivergent children have seen a certified music or art therapist who has slowly integrated the creative arts into therapy sessions, the children have improvements in social interactions and in body awareness and functions (Bernier et al., 2022).

Specific research on music therapy shows that it has potential benefits for neurodivergent children in the areas of:

- Improved social skills and communication
- Improving self-expression and creativity
- Improving emotional regulation and expression
- Increasing cognitive skills such as memory and focus
- Improving sensory integration
- Improving motor skills and coordination (AdinaABA, 2025; Stone, n.d.)

Individualized research on art therapy has shown the potential benefits for neurodivergent children include:

- Improvement in social growth and group activities
- Improvement on a child's individual strengths
- Participation whether the child is verbal or nonverbal
- Improvement of communication skills
- Desensitization of the nervous system to participate in more sensory activities (Bernier et al., 2022)

Art and Music Therapy as a Resource

Seeing a certified art or music therapist would be something that a family would do for their child as part of their medical treatment plan; however, a teacher can easily consult with an art or music therapist to learn ideas for classroom activities that can benefit neurodivergent children and typically developing children, based on the age range and ability level of the students. It is also possible that the child's IEP may include time with the school's mental-health specialist. The school guidance counselor could easily incorporate some art and music activities into the child's therapy services, then share those activities with the teacher for use in the classroom setting.

If families of neurodivergent children are looking for resources for their children, the teacher or guidance counselor can describe different types of therapeutic treatments that are available to children in their area. Organizations such as the American Music Therapy Association or the American Art Therapy Association can help locate providers in local communities when parents are looking for a specific type of therapist.

Classroom Activities

After seeing the results that music and art therapy can have on neurodivergent children, many classroom teachers would like to implement more art and music activities in their classrooms. This is a list of activities that are appropriate for preschool and elementary school students.

- **Freeze Dance:** As described in chapter 6, the children's musicians Greg and Steve (https://www.gregandsteve.com) have a wonderful song called "The Freeze." The singers tell the children when to dance and when to stop based on when the music stops. Teachers can do something similar in their classroom with a variety of music. Using different genres of music, encourage the children to dance fast or slow, smooth or choppy. Then, when the teacher pauses the music, all the children must freeze in their positions.
- **Drum circle:** A drum circle allows multiple children to participate to create a social activity. Each child has a drum. The leader of the drum circle would bang out a rhythm, and the other members of the group would attempt to copy the same rhythm. Children would take turns being the leader and having the other children copy their patterns. This could also be adapted to a singing circle where one child sings a melody, and other children copy the melody (or the tone of voice).

- **Musical storytelling:** This could be done in a large or small group. Different children take turns telling part of a story (such as a fairy tale), but they tell only a small part of the story. When each child gets up to tell their portion, they sing that part of the story. If it is a scary part of the story, the child may use a small, timid voice. If the part of the story involves a villain, then the child may use a scary voice. Children in the group have the opportunity to pass if they would rather just listen to the others tell the story, but each child has the opportunity to tell part of the story until it is complete.
- **Wind music:** The teacher can bring empty glass bottles to school and partially fill up the bottles with water at differing levels. Then, the teacher demonstrates to the children that blowing across the top of the bottle creates a tone. Each bottle has a slightly different tone since each bottle is filled with a different level of water. The children can take turns blowing on the bottles to imitate the sound of the wind or other sounds that the bottles may remind them of.
- **Match the Beat:** This game can be played in several different ways, but it is a great time to introduce body percussion. Children can create rhythm patterns with mouth sounds, slapping or clapping, then other members of the class try to match the beat. Another variation of this activity is to play a short excerpt of music and see if the children can match the beat of the music after it is turned off. This requires the children to listen carefully while the music is playing.
- **Design an album cover for your music:** This activity involves visual art and music. Select a piece of music that the class has listened to several times, then challenge the children to decorate an album cover that describes the music that will be on the album.
- **Painting to the music:** This activity not only has art and music components, but it is an excellent sensory experience. Provide painting materials in the art area. Turn on some music, then invite the children to paint what the music feels like. Offer a variety of paint colors, so children can choose colors that match the mood of the music.
- **Creating sound effects:** Although each classroom should have access to a collection of instruments that children can experiment with, children can also experiment with the sounds that they can make with their voices. Show the children pictures of items such as a rubber ball or a spring, then ask them to make a sound with their voice that reminds them of the picture.
- **Back-and-forth singing:** Some children's songs are designed as call and response, meaning the leader sings and the rest of the children respond. These include "Down By the Bay," "My Aunt Came Back," and "Old MacDonald Had a Farm." These songs have conversational patterns where individuals take turns singing just like people take turns in a conversation. Children can also create their own call-and-response songs by singing back and forth to one another in a conversation.

- **Improvisation:** Set out instruments such as a glockenspiel (a small xylophone) with color-coded keys or children's handbells that come in different colors. These instruments typically come with song sheets that show the children how to play a song based on the color bar they must strike on the glockenspiel or the color bells they must ring. This can be an introductory step for children to understand that musicians read music the same way that a student reads a book. Although the cards can be helpful for the children to practice a song, it is also important for children to know that they have the freedom to make up music as it is playing. This process is called *improvising*. Children should have the freedom to play in a way that expresses their emotions, even if it is not a song that the child already knows.
- **Student conductors:** The conductor stands in front of a choir or orchestra and directs the musicians to sing and play as one, choosing the speed and the flow of the music. Children can take turns playing the conductor. One child can stand in front of their peers and direct the other children to sing the same song. The conductor can move their arms to direct the children sing faster or slower. If the conductor uses choppy movements, then the children can sing in a short, detached manner, or if the conductor uses more fluid movements, the children can sing in a smooth voice. This same activity can be performed by passing out instruments to each child and having the lead child conduct instrumentalists instead of singers. Children can decline being the conductor, but all students should be offered the opportunity.
- **Therapeutic listening:** Therapeutic listening is a technique that music therapists use when they think a child could benefit hearing a specific piece of music. For example, if a child has been dysregulated and overly emotional, it may help for that child to listen to a calming piece of music in a relaxing area of the room. Similarly, teachers can invite a child to listen to music to help the child self-regulate and eventually feel calm enough to rejoin the class.
- **Mask making:** This visual art activity allows children the opportunity to think about how they perceive the personality and temperament of others when creating masks of different people. Although it involves a large number of art materials (such as markers, tape, glue, stickers, and construction paper), it is a reflective activity. The children could even use the opportunity to make masks of themselves.
- **Sand art:** Playing with sand offers sensory stimulation, as well as a calming effect. One way to complete sand art is to have a large tray of sand available in the art area where children can draw pictures with their fingers. When they are finished, they can gently shake the tray from side to side, and then the sand is ready for the next person. Another way to use sand art is to have the children use paintbrushes to paint a picture with liquid glue on their papers. Then, the children can shake sand on top of the glue to

create the shape of the object the children painted. As the glue dries, it will become transparent, and only the figure made with sand will be visible.

- **Ice drawing:** The teacher can freeze ice cubes with different colors and combinations of food coloring in them. It is also helpful to place an ice-pop stick in each ice cube, so once it is frozen, it basically has a handle. At the art table, the children can slide the colored ice cubes over paper to create a picture. As the ice cube melts, it will color the paper just like paint does.
- **Playdough sculptures:** When a child works with playdough or clay, it helps to develop fine motor skills and allows the child to use deep pressure with the art medium. Take this activity further by inviting the children to use the dough or clay to make a permanent sculpture. This will let them to share their work with others.
- **Fingerpaint:** Although some children are sensory-defensive to using fingerpaint, children who crave tactile sensory input can't get enough of fingerpainting. In fact, for these children, the teacher may need to watch them closely to make sure that they don't paint their whole bodies.
- **Nature art:** Invite the children to use found natural materials to create visual artwork. These materials offer a variety of colors, textures, and patterns children can use when they are creating.
- **Creating puppets:** Invite the children to make their own puppets. They can have the creative freedom to make their puppets look however they want them to look. Using the puppets with their classmates offers opportunities for social communication as they act out a story.
- **Collage and mixed media:** Completing a collage with a variety of different materials (tissue paper, beads, newsprint, magazine clippings, and so on) gives children a range of ways to express their emotions and replicate the world around them.
- **Creating a story from artwork:** For this activity, bring a print of a famous artwork, such as Van Gogh's *Starry Night*. Without giving the children any background on why the artist made the artwork, ask the children what they think is happening in the picture. The children can then make up a story about the picture with the details they have collected. The teacher can transcribe the story for the class so the children can keep the story in the book area.
- **Calming colors:** When a child is emotional or having a slightly dysregulating day, the teacher can ask if they would like to make a calming picture. Allow the child to select the colors that they think will assist them with calming down. The picture can be painted or drawn with other media.
- **Self-portraits:** Self-portraits often tell a great deal about how the child feels about herself. The portrait can be created on construction paper, or the teacher can trace an outline of the child on bulletin board paper for the child to create a life-sized self-portrait. After the child is finished with the art, the teacher can ask questions such as, "Why you are smiling in this

picture?" or "Why did you decide to draw yourself in those clothes?" to have the child describe details of the picture.

Challenges of Art and Music Therapy

Although there are definite benefits to music and art activities in the classroom, teachers may face a few challenges when implementing these strategies. First, many neurodivergent children are sensitive to sensory stimuli. Different children have different triggers. Music activities can negatively affect children who are defensive to auditory sensory input. Art activities also can have a negative effect on students who struggle with visual and tactile sensory input. One of the first things to keep in mind is not to overwhelm students with too many new activities that could cause them stress. Gradually implement new art and music techniques into the classroom, and always give children the opportunity to decline participation.

Teachers can make accommodations to most of the activities that are listed this chapter. For example, instead of fingerpainting, the teacher can offer the child a paintbrush or another tool such as a toothbrush to paint with instead of touching the fingerpaint. In group music activities, a child should have the option just to listen instead of participating in making music. If the activity is still too loud, then the child should have the option to wear noise-cancelling headphones or sit in a different part of the classroom where the music is not as loud. After some exposure to planned activities, the child may eventually want to participate.

Another obstacle is that children can quickly use up consumable materials during art activities. Knowing that classroom budgets are often quite small, sometimes families can donate art supplies. If the class is doing art with open-ended materials such as paper-towel tubes, magazine clippings, bubble wrap, and other disposable materials, ask families to save these items for the classroom instead of throwing them away at home. Asking for family donations can be a way to involve family members who wish they could volunteer in some way despite a busy work schedule. The children also feel a sense of pride when their families contribute to their classroom.

Next, we are going to change directions for a different type of educational strategy. Many children who struggle to establish social relationships with their peers may still have the ability to connect emotionally with animals. Because a strong bond with an animal can help a child develop social and emotional skills, chapter 9 will explore what that can look like in a classroom setting.

CHAPTER 9:

Animal-Assisted Therapy

The previous chapters describe many different ways teachers can help neurodivergent children feel more comfortable in the classroom setting, including integrating dance, mindful practices, and art and music therapy. Another method that has proven successful is to bring in therapy animals to help with the child's social-emotional development as well as cognitive skills (Alliance of Therapy Dogs, 2022). Therapy animals are different from service dogs, so it is important to begin by understanding what a therapy animal is and how it supports children.

What Is Animal-Assisted Therapy?

The American Veterinary Medical Association defines *animal-assisted therapy* as "a goal-directed intervention in which an animal meeting specific criteria is an integral part of the treatment process" (American Veterinary Medical Association [AVMA], 2025a). The interventions are designed to help the physical, social, emotional, or cognitive development of the individual receiving support from the animal. The therapy can also be geared toward a group, as well as just one person. The animal is there to increase the quality of life for the individual(s) by assisting with mental health, education, or recreation. This type of therapy can be used in the classroom or in medical settings.

The therapy animal's handler works in the health care or human services field and understands the needs of the individuals the animal will be supporting (AVMA, 2025a). Having a well-trained handler is as important as having a well-trained therapy animal. Since the animals are working with children to achieve specific goals, the handler needs to understand the child's needs and how to achieve the goal. This also means that animal-assisted therapy is completely different from a teacher or school employee who decides to bring a pet to school to benefit the children.

Dogs and horses are the most common animals used for animal-assisted therapy, but it is also possible to use cats, fish, guinea pigs, or other animals that could meet the screening criteria (Giorgi, 2024). Animals trained for this type of therapy must have a temperament to be around people and should not be aggressive. The animal needs polite leash skills. Therapy animals do not have the same rights as service animals. Therapy animals are not automatically allowed into buildings, so there must be an agreement in place to make sure that the facility and its administration are comfortable with the animal being on the premises and interacting with individuals. The animal must have all of the necessary vaccines and be physically able to interact with those receiving therapy. It is possible for a disabled animal to be a therapy animal (AVMA, 2025b). For example, an amputee animal may still be effective as a therapy animal.

Just as important as the therapy animal's training, the animal-assisted therapist or handler must also go through an accredited training and certification process. Training programs in animal-assisted therapy teach content including:

- Working with animals in clinical settings such as schools and medical facilities
- Interpreting the animal's body language
- Understanding the animal's emotions and its mental capacity
- Maintaining the animal's health and safety
- Creating safe therapy environments for patients
- Working with different personality types
- Learning to resolve possible problem scenarios
- Setting goals for the therapy that the animal can assist with (AVMA, 2025b)

The Benefits of Animal-Assisted Therapy

Because animal-assisted therapy diligently sets goals and evaluates the effectiveness of the interventions to meet those goals, there are documented studies of how this type of therapy can be used as a benefit (Pandey et al., 2024). The mental-health benefits of animal-assisted therapy are well documented; however, those are not the only benefits that have been established (Koukourikos, Georgopoulou, Kourkouta, and Tsaloglidou, 2019). Overall benefits include:

- Stress reduction
- Decreased levels of anxiety and depression
- Enhanced social emotional skills
- Improved communication skills
- Improved emotional regulation
- Better anger management skills
- Improved physical activity levels
- Improved cardiovascular health
- Increased cognitive function

In school-based settings, the benefits also included:

- Improved attendance rates
- Increased classroom engagement
- Improved academic performance

Students who enjoy working with a therapy animal are more interested in coming to school when they know they get to spend time with the animal. Interacting with a therapy animal is particularly rewarding for students who have a difficult time forming relationships with other children. Once a child is excited to attend school and engage in intervention, then classroom engagement and improved academic performance tend to follow.

Animal-Assisted Therapy and the Neurodivergent Mind

Although many neurodivergent individuals struggle with social relationships, some evidence suggests that neurodivergent children and adults relate better to animals than to people (Ang and MacDougall, 2022). Researchers have also conducted studies on how neurodivergent children relate to animal-assisted therapy. Several benefits stood out, including:

- Neurodivergent children engaged more in interventions with a therapy animal present.
- Therapy animals caused a calming effect for neurodivergent children.
- Working with a therapy animal improved communication skills and social behaviors (Ang and MacDougall, 2022).

Even in settings where animal-assisted therapy has not been used with neurodivergent children, it is easy to compare the challenges that these children experience to the benefits of animal-assisted therapy.

Challenges for Neurodivergent Children	Benefits of Animal-Assisted Therapy
• Difficulty with communication skills • Difficulty with social relationships • Difficulty with self-regulation	• Improved communication skills • Prosocial behaviors • Improved self-regulation • Better anger-management skills • Addressing challenging behaviors such as aggression

Seeing how this therapy not only can benefit children with so many of their challenges as well as encourage them to attend school should lead schools to consider their options for nontraditional classroom techniques.

Animal-Assisted Therapy as a Resource

Setting up animal-assisted therapy in a preschool or elementary school environment takes a great deal of planning. To make the experience beneficial for the children, the therapy must be goal-oriented and have specific interventions planned based on the child's ability level and the animal's capability to assist. To make this possible, the planning must start well in advance.

The school needs to determine its policy on therapy animals and how to support animal-assisted therapy in the educational setting. For a public school, this may mean that policy changes go through the local school board or through a school's decision-making committee. In a preschool or private-school setting, an administrative board may need to review all policies before they are implemented and may consider changes to the school's insurance or how the school will handle allergy issues.

Once the district- and school-level policies are established, the teacher needs to set up protocols. This can include answers to questions such as the following:

- How frequently does the therapy animal visit the classroom, and how long is each visit?
- Do the other children have certain rules about how to interact with the therapy animal?
- What information do families need before the therapy animal begins to visit?
- What will be the classroom protocols to make sure that the animal and the children remain safe at all times?

If the school is planning to partner with an outside agency to provide animal-assisted therapy, then the agency may already have recommended protocols. If the school is starting its own program, it must outline all protocols before the therapy begins.

The next step is for the school to identify a qualified handler and therapy animal. It could be that a staff member at the school goes through training and certification with a personal pet, or the school may choose to outsource the process and partner with an agency that specifically performs animal-assisted therapy. The animal needs experience in an education setting and in working with young children.

Once the handler and animal have been selected, set up goals for using animal-assisted therapy. Why is the animal working with the student? What goals should be complete by the end of therapy? The goals can be broader than the actual activities themselves. For example, the goal may be to improve a child's reading proficiency. The handler will plan specific activities that will focus on the child interacting with the animal while working on skills that will improve reading skills, such as reading to the animal.

For the therapy animal to help the children, a bond must be established between the children and the animal. The children need to begin to interact with the animal during classroom time, following the classroom rules about how to treat the animal when it visits. The animal also needs to trust and bond with the children so the children can assist in taking care of the animal, such as feeding it, grooming it, or taking it for walks. Therapy can begin during this bonding time, but it will be more effective once a bond is established. If a child is initially intimidated by or afraid of the animal, it will take repeated visits with the animal to establish a bond. It is best to introduce the animal toward the beginning of the school year to acclimate the animal as a typical part of the classroom. Since the first few weeks of the school year are already used to develop routines, the child will lose less potential therapy time than if the animal is introduced later in the academic year.

After interventions begin, continuously assess the child's progress toward the overall goal. If the child is not progressing after becoming acclimated to the animal, then the intervention activities should be changed. If the child surpasses this goal, a new, more challenging goal should be established. Also, it is important to assess the effect on the class as a whole and determine if any of the classroom protocols need to be changed to make sure that the children's productivity and classroom engagement is not affected when the therapy animal visits.

Classroom Activities

When the animal is first introduced, the primary focus should be on bonding with the animal and the children, so activities may focus on feeding, grooming, and spending time with the animal. As the animal and the children get more comfortable, then the animal can be more involved in curriculum-based activities. Social-emotional goals, such as building confidence and reducing anxiety or depression, may be achieved simply by letting the children spend time with the animal. In that case, the structured goal might not include implementing academic interventions. The social and emotional component is particularly important for neurodivergent children, since it is likely that their established IEP goals focus on social-emotional development also. Other activities that can be introduced include:

- Spending a set amount of time with the animal each visit
- Playing tug of war with the animal (increases engagement and arousal)

- Reading to the animal (without the judgment of peers listening)
- Having the animal sit next to the child while they complete seat work
- Playing toss and catch games with the animal to improve eye-hand coordination
- Dressing up in the dramatic play area and pretend play with the animal
- Teaching the animal to look at the child in the eyes (with a treat as a reward)
- Hiding a treat or toy and having the animal find it (problem-solving skills)
- Practicing stop-and-go activities with the animal to show that the animal is listening to the child
- Allowing the child to talk to the animal when they are upset about a situation that has occurred in the classroom
- Asking the child to teach the animal about sharing, taking turns, or other social-emotional skills
- Having the animal hold still while the child draws a picture of it
- Taking the animal on a walk down the hallway for a movement break
- Writing sight words on individual pieces of paper, getting the animal to select one (touch it), then asking the child to read the word
- Creating an obstacle course for the animal with tunnels, hoops, or block walls
- Having a larger animal such as a dog wear a vest with Velcro attached so a nonverbal child can use picture cards attached to the vest to communicate with others in the class
- Teaching the animal tricks, such as turning on the light switch or closing the door
- Hiding treats in a small rug and teaching the animal to unroll the rug to find the treats
- Resting with the animal in the classroom quiet space.

Many of these activities could fit under multiple goals, and it is also possible to find new and creative activities to support the goals that the animal-assisted therapist has designed.

Challenges of the Animal-Assisted Therapy

Although animal-assisted therapy has consistently documented benefits, it can be one of the more complicated and costly therapies to implement in the classroom setting. For public schools that receive federal funding for special education, this type of therapy might be covered by the school if it aligns with district policy and can benefit multiple children. In preschool and private-school settings, it may depend on the school's access to a therapy animal or if the family covers the cost of the therapy. The other cost is related to liability insurance. If the school partners with an outside agency, then the agency probably carries its own insurance for its animals and handlers. If the school decides to have a school therapy dog that is trained by a staff member, then the school will need to contact its insurance agent to see what adjustments need to be made to the insurance policy.

The first thing to consider when deciding if animal-assisted therapy is suitable for the classroom is whether any of the children have allergies. The health and safety of the class as a whole is the top priority, so making sure that the medical needs of all children are being met must come first. Also, consider the sanitation practices when the animal visits. For example, if a therapy dog is brought to school for the day, is there a healthy and safe plan for taking the dog outside and a plan for cleanup if the dog were to have an accident in the classroom? Although true therapy dogs (not household pets) are well trained, it's still possible the animal could have an accident.

One barrier many schools have experienced with implementing animal-assisted therapy is parental and staff buy-in. Families or staff members may be skeptical about having a therapy animal in the school for a variety of reasons, but the most common concern is that a child (or a staff member) is afraid of the animal or fears getting bitten. One of the best ways to address these concerns is to explain to families and staff that the dog and the handler must go through a rigorous training program to be certified. It is also important that any therapy animal working at the school has previous experience in a school setting and in a classroom full of children. A positive history of experiences with young children and extensive training can make parents feel much more comfortable. Schools can also offer parents the opportunity to observe in a classroom where the therapy animal is working with children to see what the interactions look like and better understand the process. If one family is adamantly opposed to their child being around the therapy animal, it is possible to arrange classroom schedules and rosters so the child does not encounter the therapy animal.

Finally, the school must use a trainer who is attentive to the interactions between the children and the animal. The trainer should ensure that the animal interacts appropriately with the children while making sure that the children interact appropriately. If certain children tease the animal, at some point the animal could react more aggressively than anticipated. In the classroom setting, it is key that the therapy animal never be pushed to that point of frustration. It is also essential that handlers make sure to watch the animal's responses to being handled by the children. Especially if the therapy animal is younger and newer to the role, it may still be adjusting to the level of attention that children offer the animal. A skilled handler can watch body language and mild responses to make sure that the animal and the children are comfortable at all times.

The strategies and practices explored so far—dance and movement, mindfulness, art and music therapy, and animal-assisted therapy—highlight the many ways educators can support neurodivergent children. It is also equally important to nurture children's ability to advocate for themselves. Self-advocacy helps children understand their needs, build confidence, and navigate school. The next chapter explores how educators can help develop students' self-advocacy skills.

CHAPTER 10:

Teaching Self-Advocacy

Children should have the opportunity to speak up for themselves. Unfortunately, children with exceptional needs are often the ones that adults overlook. It may not be intentional. Teachers and caregivers may know that a child has a disability and may assume that they need more help than the typical child. That information might lead the adults to believe the child does not know what they need, especially when a child is nonverbal or cannot read or write independently. Despite the accommodations that many children with disabilities may have, they still have the ability to communicate their needs. Because children know their own needs better than anyone else, they need to learn to be their own advocates. In this chapter, we explore ways to support children in expressing their needs.

What Is Self-Advocacy?

Self-advocacy is ability of children to communicate their wants and needs to others (Claney, 2024). It is also the children's ability to communicate their rights to teachers and caregivers so appropriate accommodations can be made. The Autistic Self Advocacy Network (ASAN, 2025) uses the phrase "nothing about us without us." They use this to speak about the autism community as a whole and to request that any decisions about policy or treatment of autistic individuals should include members of the autism community. The same general principle can be applied to the self-advocacy of a neurodivergent child. Children's voices are important, and their requests should be considered by those making decisions for them.

First, everyone should have the right to communicate their opinions. Even toddlers tell parents what they want and do not want. The same right of communication should be granted to every individual, even if they are nonverbal or communicate with assistance. Second, when a parent is making a decision for a neurodivergent child, the parent may not have experienced the medical condition or the diagnosis that the child has. The parent doesn't know what the child is struggling with or what the child is anxious about unless they talk directly to the child. Collecting this valuable information is essential. Third, once children attend child care or enter the K–12 school system, the parent is not with the child every moment of the day. Children must learn to be their own advocates and speak up for what they need, even when families are not present to be their advocates. This process of learning to protect their individual rights and meet their needs is lifelong, but it must begin early to ensure that they get the same opportunities as typically developing children in their schools and communities (Gallery, 2023).

The Benefits of Self-Advocacy

When children learn self-advocacy at a young age, it can start to show immediate benefits. Children who begin advocating for themselves have a higher level of self-confidence (Martinelli, 2025). They have been told that their rights and opinions matter, so naturally they feel that they have something important to say. Gaining this self-confidence allows children to be more likely to advocate for themselves again. It is empowering to be able to speak up for yourself, no matter what age you are.

Teaching self-advocacy also gives children the opportunity to think positively about the things they want to be successful (Gensic, 2015). Since neurodivergent children already have a strength for innovation, when we ask them to express what they need, they also have the ability to tell the adults around them how they might be able to overcome their challenges. By asking these children to use their voices, they are bringing new and creative ideas to the table.

Teaching self-advocacy also promotes acceptance and independence (Gensic, 2015). It speaks volumes when we embrace people's disabilities and still offer them the opportunity to be independent individuals. Again, there will be times when neurodivergent children can not handle a situation on their own, but when teachers and parents include children's voices in the decision-making process, it shows that children's opinions and ideas are valued. Everyone, regardless of ability, should be given that level of respect.

Developing Self-Advocacy Skills

Self-advocacy for a neurodivergent child starts with understanding the diagnosis. For very young children, this can mean the parent reads them a picture book that explains what autism is. There are wonderful picture books such as *All My Stripes: A Story for Children with Autism* by Shaina Rudolph and Danielle Royer, *The Girl Who Thought in Pictures: The Story of Dr. Temple Grandin* by Julia Finley Mosca, or *I See Things Differently: A First Look at Autism* by Pat Thomas, that begin to explain the condition in a simple manner. For elementary-age students reading chapter books, they might enjoy *Anything But Typical* by Nora Raleigh Baskin, *Rules* by Cynthia Lord, *Slug Days* by Sara Leach, and *The Earth Is Blue* by Nicole Panteleakos. Once children begin to understand the diagnosis, families should help them understand the vocabulary. Again, a neurodivergent condition will look slightly different for each child, but when children are introduced to the diagnosis, it is important to understand how the disability affects them and how it makes their daily life different.

As children become older, they should be able to identify the strengths of the neurodivergent condition as well as the challenges. It is particularly important to be able to express to teachers and caregivers what is challenging them so the adults caring for them can make the accommodations that they need to be successful. For children who struggle with verbal communication, they need to find a way to communicate with others besides their parents and primary teacher, since there will be times when it is critical to ask others for help.

When children first learn about their disability, they are also learning to accept their differences, which can be overwhelming. Many children can identify that they are different from their peers before being given the specific vocabulary defining their differences. A level of acceptance must come with knowing the exact diagnosis and understanding that the diagnosis is permanent. Many children will go through a period of time when they do not want to discuss their condition or may even ignore or refuse treatment as a way to attempt to be "normal." Part of the self-advocacy process is allowing children to experience denial, anger, bargaining, depression, and so on, before they will be comfortable talking about the diagnosis and standing up for their individual needs. Remember that this grief is not a one-time episode. At different times in children's lives, they may relive these feelings of anger or denial, and they may not want to talk about the diagnosis at those times.

Even adults have a hard time identifying their strengths and their weaknesses. Children will struggle to be self-reflective at first. Families or teachers should sit down with them and ask questions about what they do well and what is harder for them. The adults can point out that it is important to let others know about these strengths and challenges so people can support them in the right way. If, for example, a child views talking to others as a strength, then they will not want someone else speaking on their behalf. The adults around them will need to know that. If they know that they have a hard time with visual stimuli, such as flashing lights, then they will need to let others know that flashing lights are overwhelming. If a lightbulb is flickering because it is close to burning out, then an adult may need to change the lightbulb or simply turn off the light until the bulb can be replaced.

Children can practice expressing their greatest needs so they can tell someone who doesn't know them that well when they need immediate assistance. If a need isn't as urgent, then it might not require practice. Children do not have to share every detail about themselves, because it can be overwhelming to people meeting them for the first time. Some of the social graces can be taught as children get older, but with young children, it is better to prepare them with the essentials first.

As neurodivergent children approach upper elementary school, they are probably ready to understand their rights. For a child with a diagnosed disability, they have certain rights under the Individuals with Disabilities Education Act (IDEA) (US Department of Education, 2025). They have a right to a free, appropriate public education. That means that students with disabilities can receive accommodations to make sure that they get the same education as children who are typically developing. Those accommodations can look different for each student. For example, if a neurodivergent child has significant anxiety, then they may need to take tests in a less stressful setting. The accommodation would be that they can take their tests in a different classroom without worrying about how much time they have left or which of their friends finishes first. They still need to take the test, but the accommodation helps to take away the stress factor, so the teacher and school can find out how much information the child actually knows instead of how scared they are of taking the test. The schools are responsible for other accommodations, such as providing one-on-one support from teachers when children need a little extra time to learn a concept.

When children are given an IEP, they should understand what their IEPs are supposed to offer them during school (US Department of Education, 2025). For example, if they are supposed to get to see an occupational therapist once a week at school, then it is helpful for them to know what to expect. This knowledge also allows them to speak up and advocate for themselves if the occupational therapist continually must reschedule therapy sessions. It is their legal right to get the services promised in their IEPs. If they are not receiving those services, then it is important for them to speak up and let their parents or primary teachers know that the IEPs are not being followed.

Classroom Activities to Support Self-Advocacy

To help prepare children to be self-advocates as they grow up, they should develop small skills as they age. Following are classroom activities that can help children prepare. Note that all children, whether neurotypical or neurodivergent, can benefit from these self-advocacy activities.

Give opportunities for children to tell you what they like and what they don't like. This can be in group activities, such as asking, "Whose favorite character was the wolf?" "Whose favorite character was one of the pigs?" when reading and discussing "The Three Little Pigs."

When children participate in group games, allow them to speak up if they think someone didn't follow the rules.

Help children identify emotions, both their own and their peers'. This could be a game with mirrors so children can see the facial expressions for *mad, happy,* and *sad*. Or the teacher could play music and have children act out emotions. Some classrooms have dolls that show different facial expressions depicting a variety of emotions. The key is helping children identify the emotion and let others know what the emotion is.

Encourage children to ask for help instead of helping them by default. Some children may only point in the direction of the teacher or a close adult, and instantly the adult knows what the child needs. Although close relationships with children can allow the children and adults to speak without words, it is important to have the children ask for help when they need it. Other adults will not know the children this well, and asking for help is a first step toward self-advocacy.

Role-play difficult situations. When children use puppets or felt-board characters or read storybooks, they can act out a story. Many neurodivergent children may not want to be the actors if they are uncomfortable communicating with peers; however, they can still learn from the activity. When a character in a storybook or a puppet encounters a tough situation, it can be beneficial for the children to role-play how they would handle it. For example, role-play someone being unfair to the main character. Then, have the children role-play the character saying, "Stop. I don't like that." These pretend play opportunities can help children navigate a situation before they live through it.

Read storybooks about role models and characters who stand up for themselves. Collaborate with the school or local librarian to find books that will benefit the age group of the children in the class.

Create a safe learning environment where children feel comfortable asking questions and have a sense of community. For children to feel comfortable speaking up, they must feel safe and respected first. Having initial classroom experiences that allow them this level of safety and comfort sets the stage for children to be more engaged and speak up in class.

Encourage each child to be independent. Give the children the freedom to make some choices on their own so they can increase their self-confidence.

Start working on opinion writing in elementary school. If children have the opportunity to write down their opinions, they are more likely to have well-developed arguments and begin to state those opinions out loud.

As the teacher, be prepared to step back and allow children to try and resolve arguments themselves. This will give children a chance to say what they want in the middle of a disagreement instead of having the teacher say it for them. If the children cannot resolve the argument independently, then step in to mediate. Make sure that each child has an opportunity to state why they are upset and speak up for themselves, then ask the children how to resolve the situation.

Involve families in the plan for self-advocacy. Let parents know how you are supporting children to be self-advocates, and challenge them to use some of the same strategies at home.

Help children learn to set boundaries. If neurodivergent children do not feel comfortable when someone hugs them, then it is important to establish that rule with others, too. Children can tell a friend that they prefer to high-five or fist-bump but don't enjoy hugs. When children have planned ahead and established boundaries in advance, it is easier to speak up for themselves in the moment.

Help children establish a community or a core group of friends. This group then becomes a support system at school. When children are connected to others, their friends will encourage the children to meet their goals and will speak up for the child when others don't acknowledge the child's needs or rights.

Set an example of advocacy. Children are more likely to value self-advocacy when they see their parents and teachers setting an example of advocacy. This may mean that teachers take an interest in special-education public policy at the local or state level to fight for better care of the students they teach. It could also mean that teachers are more involved in IEP meetings and making sure that IEPs are implemented correctly for each student. The overall goal is for children to see that parents and teachers are willing to advocate, so advocacy must be important.

Be there when children struggle to advocate for themselves. The process of self-advocacy is not easy, and it evolves over time. When children first attempt to speak up for themselves, they may not be successful. The trusted adults in the children's lives should communicate that they are there to listen, then give them advice if they request it. Children may not want the adults to step in and fix the situation, especially as they approach adolescence. Instead, they may simply want someone who can listen to them self-reflect. It is a privilege to be a trusted adult with whom children share this type of information. Just be available to hear it.

Challenges of Teaching Self-Advocacy

Self-advocacy is a challenging skill, so children may struggle when they first attempt to speak for themselves. The first obstacle for most children is self-doubt. They may be afraid to speak up because they don't feel comfortable with what they are going to say or that they should be speaking at all. It is important to allow children to practice their "script" in advance and prepare for the moment when they will need it.

Another obstacle for neurodivergent children is communication skills. Children who are verbal may still be intimidated to speak in front of others. Children who are willing to speak may have a difficult time with nonverbal communication, such as making eye contact or using appropriate facial expressions, that draws peers or adults into the conversation. Children who are nonverbal have an even larger challenge to be heard, but it does not mean that it is impossible. Trusted adults need to practice with children so they feel comfortable using communication boards or sign language to ensure that they are understood. Since a peer or adult may not be familiar with alternative communication methods, it may be best to focus on preparing children to use simple phrases to get their point across.

When communication or language barriers continue to be an obstacle, then children might ask their community or core friends to step in and advocate for them. In most cases, the people who spend the most time with these children will understand their communication systems. If someone new, such as a new teacher or a peer that the child doesn't spend much time with, doesn't understand what the child is asking for, then a member of the child's community can step in as an interpreter to advocate on the child's behalf. Before a teacher has a planned absence, it may be beneficial to work on a script with a trusted peer of the child, so a substitute teacher is assured of getting necessary information.

Another barrier can be students and teachers who do not understand the level of the child's abilities, so they automatically dismiss the child's requests. This is an issue of education, and the teacher can definitely step in to assist. Many individuals are confused or uninformed about the neurodivergent condition, and they are even more confused when the condition includes more visible symptoms such as seizures or a lack of verbal communication. When peers don't understand the child's abilities, it can be helpful to read a storybook about the condition for young children. For elementary-age children, the child may want to give a presentation on the diagnosis. If a teacher or another adult in the school is underestimating the child, then the primary teacher or special educator may want to bring this to the administrator's attention. Talk about possible professional development opportunities for the staff that could help the entire teaching team understand the child's strengths and challenges. Teachers throughout the school must understand how to have a neurodiversity-affirming classroom, since the child will grow up in the school over a number of years. Training will make sure that future teachers are prepared to support the child and use a strengths-based approach.

A huge part of teaching children to advocate for themselves is teaching parents how to help children become self-advocates. This process can only be successful when teachers and parents have a strong partnership to help the children be the best version of themselves. The next chapter focuses on helping teachers develop those partnerships.

CHAPTER 11:

Family Partnerships

As teachers work to establish the best possible learning environment for all the children in their classrooms, parents are essential to this process. Establishing a partnership and maintaining strong communication becomes even more crucial when the teacher is attempting to implement alternative curriculum structures to meet the diverse needs in the class. Many parents may have questions about why the classroom is not using a typical structure. Even changes as small as nontraditional seating may cause questions to arise if parents have only had experiences in a classroom with rows of desks and chairs. Most parents do not work in the field of education and have not read research on why these changes benefit children. Sometimes, simple communication in a newsletter or class email is enough to keep parents informed about classroom updates, but other families may want to understand that a teacher is using research-informed decision-making to create a learning environment that benefits all students.

Parents as Children's First Teachers

When the teacher is the specialist in the field and knows that parents might have very little understanding on how children learn, it can be frustrating to constantly explain their decisions to parents. The foundation for this communication is that parents are the children's first teachers. Although the teacher may spend seven hours a day with the child over the course of one school year, parents are with that child for a lifetime. They know details about the child that the teacher may never have considered. Particularly when considering neurodivergent children, the parents know how their children react to new situations and stimuli that the teacher may not have encountered yet. When the teacher explains future changes and new systems to the parents, the parents have the opportunity to inform the teacher about the child's potential reaction to new situations. This also allows the parents to discuss the changes with the child at home in preparation for the situation and to allow the child to talk in a neutral environment about how they feel about the changes. Parents can see if the changes are positively or negatively affecting the child.

Family communication is also an educational tool. If a teacher is implementing a sensory-friendly environment at school to reduce unwanted stimuli in the child's environment, this type of information can help educate the parents on the child's needs. Education from the teacher can help the parents to implement some of the same strategies in the home, both for consistency and to gain some of the same benefits that will hopefully improve in the classroom setting. Frequently, parents regularly communicate with their child's pediatrician or a medical specialist, but those specialists may focus on the child's health and not the child's behavior. Many of the strategies that the teaching team (classroom teacher, special educator, occupational therapist, and so on) may implement in the classroom will have a direct effect on the child's behavior, and the parents may need that type of support at home as well.

Accountability is an important component of parent-teacher communication. If a neurodivergent child has an IEP or a 504 Plan, then the teacher is legally accountable for making accommodations so the child can be successful (US Department of Education, 2025). If the parents are not informed about the accommodations, then the family may assume that the school is not attempting to meet the goals outlined in the special education documents. If a child does not meet the goals listed in the IEP, the parents have the right to appeal the school's course of action if reasonable accommodations were not made. If the teacher is in communication with the family about what type of reasonable accommodations are being made to offer the child a free and appropriate public education, then the family can see that the school is held accountable for their responsibility to support the child. Although the teacher is responsible for communicating with the family to help the parents understand how the school is supporting the child, there can still be obstacles that block the parents' ability to partner with the school. Teachers need to understand those obstacles to build a relationship with the family.

Obstacles to Family Involvement

All families experience obstacles when it comes to being involved in their children's school activities. Life is busy. Many jobs expect parents to perform as if they didn't have a family to take care of outside of typical working hours. Then, if families have more than one child, it can be a juggling act to get every child to each obligation and to be involved in multiple schools.

Life becomes even more complicated for families who have a child with a disability. One of the biggest barriers to parent participation can be child care. If the school offers an event that is only for parents, the parent of a child with a disability may not have appropriate child care. It is extremely difficult to find a babysitter who feels comfortable caring for a child with special needs, and many parents don't feel comfortable leaving their neurodivergent child with someone the child doesn't know well. If the school does have an event that is focused on the whole family, it can be overwhelming for the child to be at school without experiencing their normal schedule. If the school is hosting an event such as a fall festival or spring carnival, where lots of families are in attendance, then the child may be overwhelmed by the chaos and sensory stimulation of the large crowds.

Many parents of a neurodivergent child anticipate that the child will become overwhelmed during an unstructured event. The parents may have a plan for how to guide a child through a meltdown in a public place, but it can be challenging for the parent or caregiver to deal with the judgment and stigma they experience from other parents and community members. For some reason, strangers seem more than willing to offer discipline advice when a child has an emotional outburst in public. Without the knowledge of the child's disability, adults will often offer the parents advice on how to handle the child's meltdown. This type of unsolicited advice often makes the parents of neurodivergent children feel inadequate and belittled. Even worse, it is demeaning when strangers come up to the parents and make comments like, "My mother would never have allowed me to behave like that when I was his age." These types of judgments seem harsh, and they definitely do not improve the situation the parent is experiencing at the moment. Unfortunately, if you look at chat rooms and blogs of parents with neurodivergent children, you can see that parents and caregivers experience this type of criticism far more frequently than one might expect. Once parents have lived through this type of public scorn, they are much less likely to take their children out in a public setting again for some time. If parents experience this type of criticism at a school event, they may be less likely to attend similar events in the future.

If a parent grew up receiving special-education services and had a negative experience, then they may be extremely resistant to getting that type of support for their child. It was only a few decades ago that children who received any special education services were completely isolated from the rest of the school. This isolation led to children being frequently taunted because their typically developing peers didn't know anything about them and didn't have relationships with the children in the "special classroom" down the hall. Of course, mocking and bullying still exist today, but that stigma around the "special classroom" did not help children understand one another. Many parents may want to prevent their children from having those types of experiences, so they may not be willing to collaborate with any type of special-education services. Even though the structure of special education has dramatically changed, parents may not be aware of what inclusive classrooms look like today.

Chronic Sorrow

It is also important to remember that parents may have a hard time collaborating with teachers when they are dealing with their own emotions regarding their child's disability. Many parents of children with disabilities experience a condition known as *chronic sorrow* (Raap, Weille, and Dedding, 2024). This is when the parent experiences long-term, recurring grief over the course of the child's life. The parent is grieving not for the child they have but for the child they expected to have. Most parents begin dreaming about their child's life as soon as they know they are expecting. They may be dreaming of a child who will be a famous dancer, musician, or president of the United States, or they could be dreaming of a child who will follow in the family tradition of working in a particular trade, attending the same university as previous generations, or playing Major League baseball. When that child is born with, or is later diagnosed with, a disability, the parents experience a period of grief in which they mourn for the child they expected. This in no way means that the parents do not love the child they have, but it is how the parents come to terms with the life that the child will actually have.

This experience of grief will probably occur more than once as the child grows, particularly around large developmental milestones, depending on the type of disability that the child has. Some of the most common time periods that parents experience this type of grief might be as the child begins elementary school, as the child enters puberty (and other children begin dating), as the child graduates from high school (and other children pursue college and job-training programs), as peers begin to get married and have children, and as parents begin to worry about their own end-of-life care and planning for their child's future. This doesn't mean that a child who is neurodivergent won't date, go to college, have a family, or be an independent adult. It does mean that those milestones may look different for the child than the parent initially anticipated, so the parent may have to grieve over the loss of what they anticipated and learn to accept the reality that is occurring. Sometimes, these are simple losses, such as a child who refuses to go to high school dances, but it can still be emotional for the parent if they dreamed about the child experiencing these right-of-passage moments. In other cases, a child may require many more accommodations to be successful in his education and after graduating from high school.

As parents cope with these losses, they will experience the same stages of grief that a person goes through when someone close to them passes away:

- Denial
- Anger
- Bargaining
- Depression
- Acceptance

Many parents initially deny that anything is different about their children. After identifying the developmental differences in their child, parents may experience anger or attempt to bargain with the heavens and request, "If you will just make it possible for [milestone] to happen . . ." Depression is also a completely natural response to processing this type of situation. It is important for parents to understand that they may need professional support at times, just like their children do. Many parents see a mental-health counselor to process these feelings of loss and to make sure that they can focus on being the best possible parent to the child that they do have, instead of focusing on the loss. If there are other children in the home, they may also need counseling to understand and learn how to support the sibling.

Teachers or other professionals working with parents of neurodivergent children should be prepared to help families find the resources they need when they are struggling. Of course, educators do not have the background to give a mental-health diagnosis or tell a parent what type of mental-health assistance they may need. Instead, it can be useful to have a small packet of resources compiled that includes supports for the children and supports for the family as a whole. Simply letting the family know the options that are available in the local community can be a first step to helping families once they realize they need additional support.

Parental Advocacy

Parents of children with disabilities have a huge job, but one of their responsibilities includes advocating for their children. Many parents are intimidated when it comes to advocating for their children, because they naturally want to avoid confrontation; however, advocacy doesn't have to be aggressive. It is more about accountability than arguments. Teachers may feel uncomfortable with a parent who strongly advocates for their child, because the parent's advocacy makes them second-guess their decisions for the child. Ultimately, the goal is for the parent and the teacher to form a partnership to work toward the shared goal of helping the child to be successful.

To create this partnership, it can be beneficial for the teacher to document the child's progress and to share that information with the parent whenever questions arise. This does not mean that the teacher needs to document everything the child does. Instead, the focus can be more on short daily notes that allow the teacher to remember whether the child struggled with daily assignments or if additional accommodations were needed to complete a task successfully.

If the child has an IEP, then the special-education teacher will be responsible for documenting information leading up to the child's IEP goals, along with test scores and other information. Ultimately, the special-education teacher does not spend the same amount of time with the child as the classroom teacher does if the child's primary placement is in the inclusive classroom. This means that the teacher should be the expert on the child in the school setting. The documentation that can really help a parent to understand what is going on in the classroom could include the following:

- Triggers that set off challenging behaviors
- Key interactions with peers (both positive and negative)
- The level of engagement during group activities
- The level of independence during independent activities
- Subjects or activities that the child consistently struggles with
- Times of the day when the child has a difficult time
- How the child handles transitions
- Key phrases that the child uses to communicate with others

Teachers should also document date and time whenever possible, so parents understand when these challenges are occurring and how frequently they occur.

When parents see that teachers are taking an active interest in the child's progress, they typically take a problem-solving approach to their advocacy instead of simply coming in to speak to the teacher in anger. It is still important to form a plan for how to handle a parent who approaches the situation with anger. The plan may include meeting with the parent and an administrator, creating a plan with the help of the parent, and setting a follow-up meeting with the parent to see if the plan addressed the needs. Remember that if a parent is angry, it is their job to protect their children, so they are behaving that way to fight for their child. Even though it can be overwhelming to deal with an angry parent, it is a blessing for the child to have a parent who is involved, as opposed to a parent who is not concerned with their growth and development.

Self-Care and Respite

While some parents are overly involved in their children's progress, other parents are simply struggling to meet the basic needs of their families. There is a significant lack of respite care for children with special needs, which often means that parents of children with special needs are physically and emotionally exhausted (Graaf, Baiden, Keyes, and Boyd, 2022). In August 2024, the US Surgeon General released a report that expressed higher levels of stress for parents than other adults (Roeloffs, 2024). He expressed concerns that the mental health needs of parents were not being met due to the needs of their children. This report primarily focused on parents of typically developing children. Other research has shown that parents with children who have special needs have increased stress levels due to factors such as:

- additional financial burdens,
- medical needs and access to necessary health care,
- lack of appropriate child care,
- work-life balance,
- parental guilt,
- strain on the marriage and other significant relationships,
- exhaustion and burnout, and
- emotional stress on the parents and other members of the family (Cheng and Lai, 2023).

When working with families who have a child with special needs, keep in mind that the family needs a lot of support, too. These are often parents who are giving a huge amount of time to the care and protection of their child, but they have given minimal time to their own personal needs. This can look different for each family. Some parents may simply need someone to vent to, because they feel isolated from friends and family due to the complex needs of the child. Other families are struggling to balance work and caring for their children. When the school calls the parent at work, that can be a trigger for the parent to become extremely emotional if they are worried about maintaining a job after having to miss work repeatedly for the child. This is something that schools need to consider. If possible, instead of requesting the parent to come to the school frequently, be supportive about handling meltdowns and other behavior issues at the school.

Unfortunately, some families may be so stressed that the parents unknowingly may be at risk of abusive situations. Children with special needs are much more likely to be abused than typically developing children—approximately three times the rate of typically developing children (Legano et al., 2021). This can be because some children are unable to report when they have been abused, but it can also be because children with behavioral disabilities show extremely challenging behaviors. Although teachers and nannies are sometimes the abusers, there is a much higher chance that the child's parent or the parent of a parent may be the abuser. When a parent or caregiver experiences high levels of stress over a significant period of time with no break to recover emotionally, then they are more at risk of abusing a child, even when they deeply care for the child (Legano et al., 2021).

Although teachers are mandatory reporters of abuse, the goal is to notice the symptoms of stress and burnout in advance and to help support the parent or caregiver to avoid abuse altogether. Respite-care options or support groups for parents with children who have disabilities can help emotionally support parents who need a break as caregivers. Many communities have a local chapter of the American Autism Society or similar groups based on the diagnosis of the child. Hospitals or mental-health clinics may also have parent groups that focus on families with neurodivergent children. It is key for families to have a community of support, whether that is family, friends, or a community group. When families feel supported and can have breaks to care for their own needs, they are better able to care for their children with a more positive outlook.

Establishing a Parent Partnership Plan

When teachers decide to implement a new technique in the classroom, such as practicing mindfulness or using a therapy dog, these changes should start with general family education. A newsletter or a family education night provides teachers with an opportunity to describe the benefits for the whole classroom and the rationale behind the changes. This also gives parents an opportunity to express their concerns. For example, if the school is going to start using a therapy dog, then the parents of a child who is afraid of dogs may come forward with concerns at that time. The parents and the teachers can brainstorm the best way to support the child during this transition. It may be beneficial to have a plan for the dog to stay a certain distance away from the child while they get acclimated to the animal. The teacher may also want to plan certain times for the child to have supervised interaction with the dog until they are more comfortable with the animal. Once the child is more comfortable spending time with the therapy dog, then those initial accommodations may not be needed anymore.

Once the changes are implemented, then the teacher will want to communicate with the parents of the neurodivergent child to talk about the goals that the teacher would like to see for the student based on the curriculum and classroom changes. If it is possible, the family may want to implement some of those changes in the home as well to establish consistency. For example, if the teacher begins to implement mindfulness and calming practices, then the family may want to begin utilizing deep-breathing practices at home when the child starts to get overwhelmed, to reinforce the classroom strategies.

After an initial window of teaching the children about using the new strategies, then the teacher can begin to track whether the new strategies are helping the child achieve their established goals. That data can be tracked to share with the parents of the neurodivergent child to show how the changes are affecting the child. Again, this communication creates accountability between the teacher and the family to show the dedication to helping the child be successful. It also helps the parents understand how the process works to help the child learn new self-regulation skills and improve overall classroom function. To make sure that the teacher is sharing accurate information on progress with the family, it is critical that the teacher finds effective methods for tracking progress over time. We will discuss that topic in the next chapter.

CHAPTER 12:
Assessment for Tracking Progress

When a child is initially diagnosed with a neurodivergent condition, the diagnosis is typically made by a child psychologist or a medical doctor. Although the Individuals with Disabilities Education Act requires schools to do some form of re-evaluation every three years regarding the child's overall progress, that evaluation does not change the child's diagnosis (US Department of Education, 2025). The child psychologist will typically use an established tool for evaluation, such as the Autism Diagnostic Observation Schedule (ADOS), or a medical professional may use genetic testing, blood tests, or other tools to test for a medical diagnosis. After those initial tests, evaluating progress will typically be a less formal but still structured process. This chapter looks at ways that educators—with the support of families—can track the progress of children over the course of the school year to see each child meet new milestones and progress, even if the children are not meeting the developmental milestones for their chronological age due to their diagnosis.

Collecting Information

Teachers can collect data on special-education students in a variety of ways, although the most popular include observation and test scores (Swain, Hagaman, and Leader-Janssen, 2021). Depending on the age of the child, tests can have multiple meanings. For older students, tests can mean academic assessments of the content the teacher has been teaching. For young students, teachers can use a test or assessment to look at the students' developmental milestones and see if they are above or below the developmental norms for a child of the same age. Observations can look at the child's individual behaviors or at how the child interacts with others in the classroom setting. Some typical data collecting methods include the following techniques.

- **Anecdotal notes:** Anecdotal notes would include the observer (classroom teacher or a special educator) writing down a log of the behaviors the student is exhibiting. The observer would not interact with the student during this time. Instead, they would watch the child and write down each action the child performs, giving some reference to the time involved. Then, after the notes are completed, the observer could review them and look for patterns in the behaviors observed. For example, if the observer documented an emotional outburst, then they could review the notes to see what happened prior to the outburst to look for a trigger for the behavior.
- **Video recordings:** In the same way that the observer might write down anecdotal notes, a video recording could also be used to watch all the actions that occur in the classroom. The video would allow the observer to go back and rewatch segments to understand the environmental factors and what the child and others were doing. With a video recording, the staff would need parent permission of the children being recorded in the video, since there would be some privacy factors involved for all the children who were included in the video. The video would also allow other specialists (special education teacher, therapist, school psychologist, and so on) to see some of the concerning behaviors if they were not in the classroom at the same time the observation occurred.
- **Checklists and rating scales:** Checklists or rating scales are more formal tools used to specifically look at targeted behaviors or developmental milestones. Most published checklists or rating scales have been norm-referenced and used by a test group of educators to make sure that the assessment tool is accurate. The teacher also has the option of creating an individualized checklist or rating scale. In this case, the teacher may be using the tool to track the number of targeted behaviors that the student demonstrates during the assessment period. If the tool is homemade, then it is simply a different method of efficiently collecting key data while still using class time to teach lessons.

- **Graphing data trends:** The teacher might use the different forms of data collected during observations to create a line graph to show how the student has progressed or declined over time. The teacher would need to have baseline data before the classroom accommodations began to show whether or not a specific intervention has improved or hindered progress (EUNA Solutions, 2024). It is also possible to add a line in the graph that shows typical student progress to see how the child's progress compares to the norm (whether that is based on other students that age, other students in the district, and so on).

Each of these forms of data can be used for documenting growth during an IEP meeting. Also, if the child is in a private school that does not use government documents, this type of data can still help parents understand the types of behaviors that the child is exhibiting and how the educators are attempting to support the student in being successful.

Alignment with Neurodiversity-Affirming Behavior

As teachers document the behaviors and academic growth of neurodiverse students, it is important to remember how best to use this information in a neurodiversity-affirming classroom (Roberts, 2022). In this type of classroom setting, some applied behavior analysis techniques may be controversial because there is punishment involved and a desire to eliminate behaviors that may not be harmful to the child. Again, the goal is to take a strengths-based approach to learning for neurodiverse students and to support them with challenging behaviors. In this type of setting, the classroom teacher and special educator would not be working to "cure" the child. Instead, the goal would be to help the child be successful, based on the skills that they already have. While observing and assessing progress on goals, the teachers would still want to make sure to do the following:

- **Reduce masking** by allowing the child to demonstrate their unique personality. It is important not to force a neurodiverse child to exhibit neurotypical behaviors. For example, in a preschool classroom, this may mean that a neurodiverse child is not forced to sit still during circle time but is able to move around the room behind the children sitting in circle time while listening to the conversation.
- **Assess the child in a neurodiverse-affirming manner,** including using accepting language about the child's classroom behaviors, as long as the child is not harming herself or others.

- **Focus on communication goals** that allow the child to decline social interaction in a respectful way, if that is what the child needs at that time.
- **Focus on safety and personal growth** when evaluating behavior, after writing factual and neutral observations in the child's observation record.

The assessment process and the evaluation process in a neurodiversity-affirming classroom should still focus on allowing neurodiverse students to be themselves while challenging their overall development. Whether the children are performing above, at, or below the typical developmental milestones for their age, encourage each child to meet new goals and progress, so the established goals should focus on helping each individual student overcome the challenges that often prevent them from being successful.

SMART Goals

George Doran created the model for SMART goals in 1981 (Bjerke and Renger, 2017). His outline created goals that are quantifiable and ready for evaluation. His SMART goals consisted of five components:

- **Specific:** Each goal should be well-defined and not have multiple meanings. Provide details that explain who will do what and when the goal will be completed.
- **Measurable:** This means that it will be obvious if the goal is completed or not. This might be a numeric response, such as stating that the child should be able to complete the skill a certain number of tries, but it could also just describe the specific skill that needs to be completed to state whether or not the goal was achieved.
- **Achievable:** The goal should be within the reach of the child's ability with a small amount of growth. Setting the goal too high would ensure that the child would not be successful.
- **Relevant:** The goal needs to relate to progress that is beneficial for the child. Setting a goal that the child has already achieved or is unrelated to an essential skill will not benefit the child in the long run.
- **Time-bound:** The goal needs to have a specific timeline so it inspires progress and accountability (Bell, 2025).

When applying these guidelines to goals for neurodivergent children, the teacher and special-education team must look at the areas where the children struggle the most, such as:

- Communication skills
- Social interactions
- Repetitive behaviors
- Sensory stimulation
- Academic achievement
- Aggressive behaviors (Mastermind Behavior, 2024)

Since many of these areas are not scored on homework or tests, the education team must think of the behavior that they want to see increase or decrease, then determine what would be reasonable for the child to achieve.

Sample Goals for Children

Academic Goals

- By the end of the school year, Shana will complete 80 percent of each assignment before turning it in to the teacher.
- By the end of the semester, Alicion will read a three-paragraph narrative and verbally summarize the content without adult assistance.

Social Goals

- By the end of the school year, Joseph will participate in group learning activities an average of three out of five times that he is offered the opportunity. He may have up to two prompts from a teacher or peer.
- By the end of the semester, Liza will initiate an interaction with her peers three out of five times that she has the opportunity during recess or lunch time.

Behavioral Goals

- Within two months, Elijah will use a self-calming technique three out of five times he becomes upset during class time.
- Within one month, Tanay will hit a pillow or stuffed animal instead of a teacher or student when she becomes upset.

There are a few extra details to remember when setting goals for neurodivergent children. For example, children with social delays will need a break from social situations, so it is more reasonable not to set a social goal with 100 percent compliance. If a neurodivergent child is learning to self-regulate (which is the goal), they will know there are times when they should take a break from other people. In contrast, aggressive behaviors need to be eliminated as soon as possible to protect the safety of teachers and the other children. Since it may be difficult to eliminate the behavior altogether, the first step may be providing a replacement behavior where the student can safely express extreme emotions. When establishing the replacement behavior, and eventually eliminating the behavior altogether, this is one time when 100 percent compliance is the goal as soon as possible. In most educational settings, it is unusual to achieve a goal of 100 percent compliance because every child makes mistakes in academic and social skills. However, with aggressive behaviors and other actions that endanger safety, 100 percent compliance is essential to keep children safe.

Individualized Education Programs (IEPs)

The goal of each IEP is to personalize it to the student's needs. Of course, the general developmental goals of the students are used to create the IEP, but due to the sheer number of IEPs that some special educators must write each year, many goals are reused on different children's IEPs simply because the framework is already in the educator's mind. For children who simply need more practice and more repetition with reading, it may work to borrow a goal from a peer. On the other hand, if the IEP is for a neurodivergent student whose brain does not operate in the same manner as most of their peers, then it is critical to individualize the goal to the child.

The first step toward individualizing an IEP is to start with feedback from the child's family. Although the educators at the table know a great deal about the developmental norms for a child at each stage of development, the family knows about the development of that individual child. The family also knows the challenges that affect the child the most on a daily basis. The educators can offer context to the family on whether or not that particular challenge occurs as much in the classroom setting with other children around. With that combination of information, the team can identify the general areas that need the most attention.

Next, the team needs to consider creating SMART goals, but goals need to be considered within the context of a neurodiverse perspective. For example, sensory support should not be a reward. This support needs to be provided continuously for a neurodiverse child to be successful. It's a classroom accommodation that should always be in place in the environment and that applies if the child needs a reduction in sensory stimuli or an increase in sensory stimuli to be more successful. The classroom environment, such as the room arrangement, having materials accessible for the child to choose independently, or finding areas of the classroom where the child can be alone, should stay the same so children know what to expect.

When the team sets communication goals, they shouldn't strictly look at verbal communication. If a child is emotionally overwhelmed, then the IEP goals should allow for other forms of communication, such as a communication board or nonverbal communication. Verbal communication can be encouraged, but the classroom needs to be set up in a way that values different forms of communication, to show respect to all students.

When the Admissions and Release Committee (ARC)—the group that comes together to create the IEP—sets goals for completion of work, they should consider what classroom engagement looks like for the particular child. A child should not be expected to sit at a desk or on the floor and ingest information with no other alternatives. The classroom should allow for movement throughout the learning space, including times when large-group learning is happening. Children should not be required to sit in a seat to complete table work. Group work should be adapted for children who need to take short breaks. If a child is required to be engaged in large-group activities for a certain amount of time, then engagement should allow for movement and breaks when needed.

Many neurodivergent children are striving for independence. They desire to be autonomous. Although there are certain school rules that must stay in place, particularly those supporting safety and guaranteeing all children the right to an appropriate education, some rules can easily be changed to avoid unnecessary power struggles with children. Goals that state a child must choose one of two options do not allow for the possibility that a child may have their own innovative solution to a problem. Goals that state a child must be 100 percent compliant at the end of a semester or a year do not consider that a child may know that they need a break from social interaction or an opportunity to do a project independently instead of in a group. Offer opportunities for students to be independent when they need to be, and save strict compliance for issues of safety and maintaining all students' basic rights.

Frequent Monitoring

To make sure that progress is occurring, it is important for classroom teachers and special educators to use frequent monitoring. Each school or district may have a different requirement for what "frequent" monitoring requires. The key component is that a regular schedule dictates when the child will be monitored in the learning environment, and everyone on the educational team is aware of what that monitoring schedule is. For example, one school district may choose to collect data on a student once a week or biweekly. Every schedule must establish what needs to be observed so the method of observation and assessment is consistent. Also, if concerning data is collected, then the teacher must let the full educational team know that the child's IEP may need to be updated if the current accommodations are not helping the child make progress (particularly if the data collection process begins to show decline in developmental skills).

Even though the IEP may be reviewed only once a year at the child's annual ARC meeting, the members of the ARC committee should communicate frequently about the child's progress. This includes communication with the child's parents or guardians. Communication may be intermittent parent-teacher conferences or achievement reports. Of course, in elementary school the students will receive report cards, but numeric grades may not help parents understand what progress is being made on social or behavioral goals on the children's IEPs. One of the best ways to communicate progress updates is simply to email the parents when the child achieves a new skill or shows noted progress in challenging areas. These updates can be used with the educational team to make sure that all team members are seeing the same types of progress. It is also important for the educational team to share observational notes, video recordings, and checklists with one another to track overall progress and see what accommodations may be changed to help make sure that the child's annual goals are achieved.

Fidelity to Accommodations —Educator Assessment

It is essential to not only assess whether the data shows that the child is progressing toward their developmental goals but also to assess the teacher's fidelity in implementing the strategies to support growth. When an IEP is created, a section of the document lists the accommodations that the teacher and special educator will implement to help the student achieve the documented goals. If the educators do not regularly use the accommodations but the child is still assessed on progress toward the goals, then it is likely that the child will make very little progress. There would also be an issue of fidelity if the educators are regularly evaluating child data and fail to hold an IEP meeting when a child consistently is not making progress. The educator is accountable to the accommodations, or adapting the accommodations, to provide the child with the most appropriate education in the least restrictive environment—meaning the most time in the general classroom as possible to be successful (US Department of Education, 2025).

Fidelity checks should occur on a regular basis, depending on the structure of the school district and the immediate supervisors of the classroom teacher and the special-education teacher (DeLussey, 2023). The school district may use a specific checklist to ensure fidelity, or they may simply review child-progress data with accommodation information to see how the educator is implementing an IEP (IRIS Center, 2025). A fidelity checklist may look at the following:

- The amount of time a child spends with the special education teacher each week
- The amount of support services (speech therapy, occupational therapy, intervention, and so on) that the child receives each week
- The types of accommodations (such as scribing, shortening assignments, offering extra time to complete assignments) being used in the classroom and for which subjects (IRIS Center, n.d.)

When a fidelity assessment is conducted, it may reveal more information than whether or not the classroom teacher is implementing the accommodations as needed. It could show that additional school personnel are needed, based on the amount of time that each student is awarded in the special-education classroom or with support staff. That type of evaluation result can be beneficial to classroom staff who feel overwhelmed by serving so many children at one time. In other cases, the evaluation information may show that the child is receiving all the required supports and accommodations but is still not making progress. In that case, the IEP may need to be updated with a higher level of support. All of this information is important to make sure that children with special needs get the appropriate amount of support to be successful.

The Cycle of Assessment

The ultimate goal of assessment is to meet all of the established goals. In an IEP, the goal would be for the student to surpass the goals established for the current school year. Once a child achieves progress, then the cycle of assessment starts all over. New SMART goals are established for the child, with more advanced skills or with fewer supports, then the data collection process starts all over again.

The original baseline data from the student's initial diagnosis or when the IEP process began is used for comparison to track new growth. Yearlong or semester-specific data is gathered to show the student's progress or to establish that the student needs higher levels of support. This collection and evaluation process will continue to guide the education team, with parent collaboration, to find the best strategies to track child growth.

If a teacher is implementing creative strategies for a neurodiversity-affirming classroom, then the collection of data will confirm whether one of the new strategies is working or whether the teacher should try a different technique. It is also important for the teacher to track overall classroom trends before abandoning a technique that was added during this transition process. For example, if a teacher implemented techniques to teach self-advocacy, the new strategy may not work for the student who initiated the change, but there may be qualitative data to show that other students in the classroom greatly benefit from the changes. Instead of abandoning that change, perhaps a new technique needs to overlap with that technique for the benefit of all the students. Continued research on new strategies to support the children with a structured evaluation system will ultimately help provide the best educational environment for the entire classroom community.

REFERENCES AND RECOMMENDED READING

AdinaABA. 2024. "The Best Music Therapies to Unlock Progress for Individuals with Autism." AdinaABA. https://www.adinaaba.com/post/best-music-therapies-for-autism

Alcorn, Alyssa M., et al. 2024. "Learning about Neurodiversity at School: A Feasibility Study of a New Classroom Programme for Mainstream Primary Pupils." *Neurodiversity* (2). SagePub Open Access. https://journals.sagepub.com/doi/full/10.1177/27546330241272186

Alliance of Therapy Dogs. 2022. "How Do Therapy Dogs Help in the Classroom?" Alliance of Therapy Dogs. https://www.therapydogs.com/how-do-therapy-dogs-help-in-the-classroom/

Ang, Chin-Siang, and Freya Anne MacDougall. 2022. "An Evaluation of Animal-Assisted Therapy for Autism Spectrum Disorders: Therapist and Parent Perspectives." *Psychological Studies* 67(1): 72–81. doi: 10.1007/s12646-022-00647-w

American Art Therapy Association. 2022. "About Art Therapy." American Art Therapy Association. https://arttherapy.org/about-art-therapy/

American Montessori Society. 2024. "What Is Montessori Education?" American Montessori Society. https://amshq.org/About-Montessori/What-Is-Montessori

American Psychiatric Association. 2022. *Diagnostic and Statistical Manual of Mental Disorders, Text Revision*. 5th edition. Washington, DC: American Psychiatric Association.

American Psychiatric Association. 2025. "What Is ADHD?" American Psychiatric Association. https://www.psychiatry.org/patients-families/adhd/what-is-adhd

American Psychological Association. 2025. "Mindfulness." American Psychological Association. https://www.apa.org/topics/mindfulness

American Veterinary Medical Association. 2025a. "Animal-Assisted Interventions: Definitions." AVMA. https://www.avma.org/resources-tools/avma-policies/animal-assisted-interventions-definitions

American Veterinary Medical Association. 2025b. "Animal-Assisted Interventions: Guidelines." AVMA. https://www.avma.org/resources-tools/animal-health-and-welfare/service-emotional-support-and-therapy-animals/animal-assisted-interventions-guidelines

Anderson, Jeffrey T., et al. 2024. "A Novel Dance Intervention Program for Children and Adolescents with Developmental Disabilities: A Pilot Randomized Control Trial." *BMC Sports Science, Medicine, and Rehabilitation*. 16: 109. doi: 10.1186/s13102-024-00897-3

Anixter, William, and Courtney Kelly. 2023. "The Benefits of Plant and Animal Caretaking for Individuals with Autism." Psychology Today. https://www.psychologytoday.com/us/blog/a-healing-community/202305/the-benefits-of-plant-and-animal-caretaking-for-individuals-with

Anzilotti, Amy W. 2023. "504 Education Plans." Nemours KidsHealth. https://kidshealth.org/en/parents/504-plans.html#:~:text=What%20Is%20a%20504%20Plan,504%20of%20the%20Rehabilitation%20Act

APA Member Services. 2023. "Strength in Neurodiversity." American Psychological Association. https://www.apa.org/members/content/neurodiversity

Arky, Beth. 2025. "Calm Voices, Calmer Kids." Child Mind Institute. https://childmind.org/article/calm-voices-calmer-kids/#:~:text=Addressing%20inappropriate%20behavior%20calmly%20enables,how%20to%20self%2Dregulate%20themselves

Ashinoff, Brandon K., and Ahmad Abu-Akel. 2019. "Hyperfocus: The Forgotten Frontier of Attention." *Psychological Research* 85(1): 1–19. doi: 10.1007/s00426-019-01245-8

Austin, Robert D., and Gary P. Pisano. 2017. "Neurodiversity as a Competitive Advantage." Harvard Business Review. https://hbr.org/2017/05/neurodiversity-as-a-competitive-advantage

Autistic Self Advocacy Network. 2025. "What We Believe." ASAN. https://autisticadvocacy.org/about-asan/what-we-believe/

Ayres, Amir T. 2023. "3 Ways to Ensure Teacher Buy-In for Big Changes." Edutopia. https://www.edutopia.org/article/ensure-teacher-buy-in-big-changes/

Bauer, Emily. 2024. "The Importance of Adopting a Neurdiversity Affirming Approach: A Training for School Counselors." Masters thesis, Minnesota State University, Moorhead. https://red.mnstate.edu/thesis/974/

Bauld, Andrew. 2021. "Make Outdoor Learning Your Plan A." Harvard Graduate School of Education. https://www.gse.harvard.edu/ideas/usable-knowledge/21/08/make-outdoor-learning-your-plan#:~:text=Research%20has%20shown%20that%20outdoor,There%20are%20challenges

Bell, Simon. 2025. SMART Goals. MindTools. https://www.mindtools.com/a4wo118/smart-goals

Bergman, Erin. 2024. "Autism and Dancing: What Are the Benefits?" Autism Parenting. https://www.autismparentingmagazine.com/dance-movement-benefits/#:~:text=There%20are%20many%20dance%20programs%20geared%20specifically%20toward%20kids%20with,just%20as%20beneficial%20and%20fun

Bernier, Allison, et al. 2022. "Art Interventions for Children with Autism Spectrum Disorder: A Scoping Review." *American Journal of Occupational Therapy* 76(5): 7605205030. doi: 10.5014/ajot.2022.049320

Bjerke, May Britt, and Ralph Renger. 2017. "Being Smart about Writing SMART Objectives." *Evaluation and Program Planning* 61: 125–127.

Broder-Fingert, Sarabeth, and Danielle Abate. 2022. "Embracing Neurodiversity in Our Health Systems." AAP Voices Blog. https://www.aap.org/en/news-room/aap-voices/embracing-neurodiversity-in-our-health-systems/#:~:text=The%20term%20neurodiversity%20describes%20the,they%20can%20be%20important%20strengths

Brown, Lydia. 2011. "Identity-First Language." Autistic Self Advocacy Network. https://autisticadvocacy.org/about-asan/identity-first-language/

Buss, Kristin A. 2024. "The Role Parents Play in Shaping Children's Emotion Regulation." Psychology Today. https://www.psychologytoday.com/us/blog/growing-hearts-and-minds/202406/the-role-parents-play-in-shaping-childrens-emotion-regulation

Cabrera, Natasha, et al. 2022. *Rebalancing: Children First.* https://www.brookings.edu/articles/rebalancing-children-first/

Calderon, Johanna. 2020. "Executive Function in Children: Why It Matters and How to Help." Harvard Health Publishing. https://www.health.harvard.edu/blog/executive-function-in-children-why-it-matters-and-how-to-help-2020121621583

California State Council on Developmental Disabilities. n.d. *The Difference between IEPs and 504 Plans*. https://scdd.ca.gov/wp-content/uploads/sites/33/2018/03/The-Difference-Between-IEP-and-504-Plans.pdf

Center on the Developing Child. 2025. "Brain Architecture." Center on the Developing Child at Harvard University. https://developingchild.harvard.edu/key-concept/brain-architecture/

Centers for Disease Control and Prevention. 2023. "Autism Prevalence Higher, According to Data from 11 ADDM Communities." CDC Newsroom. https://www.cdc.gov/media/releases/2023/p0323-autism.html

Centers for Disease Control and Prevention. 2024. "About Attention-Deficit/Hyperactivity Disorder (ADHD)." CDC. https://www.cdc.gov/adhd/about/index.html#:~:text=Types,inattentive%20and%20hyperactive%2Dimpulsive%20symptoms

Cheng, Andrew W. Y., and Cynthia Y. Y. Lai. 2023. "Parental Stress in Families of Children with Special Educational Needs: A Systematic Review." *Frontiers in Psychiatry* 14. https://doi.org/10.3389/fpsyt.2023.1198302

Child Mind Institute. 2025. "How Sensory Processing Issues Affect Kids in School." Child Mind Institute. https://childmind.org/article/how-sensory-processing-issues-affect-kids-in-school/#:~:text=Sensory%20processing%20issues%20can%20make,because%20their%20clothing%20is%20uncomfortable

Claney, Carly. 2024. "Self-Advocacy Strategies for Neurodivergent Adults." Relational Psych. https://www.relationalpsych.group/articles/self-advocacy-strategies-for-neurodivergent-adults#:~:text=Self%2Dadvocacy%20specifically%20relies%20on,that%20is%2C%20neurodivergent%20people%20-themselves

Cleveland Clinic. 2024. "What Is Masking? And What's the Harm?" Cleveland Clinic. https://health.clevelandclinic.org/what-is-masking

Cleveland Clinic. 2025a. "Dyscalculia." Cleveland Clinic. https://my.clevelandclinic.org/health/diseases/23949-dyscalculia

Cleveland Clinic. 2025b. "Dysgraphia." Cleveland Clinic. https://my.clevelandclinic.org/health/diseases/23294-dysgraphia

Cleveland Clinic. 2025c. "Dyspraxia." Cleveland Clinic. https://my.clevelandclinic.org/health/diseases/23963-dyspraxia-developmental-coordination-disorder-dcd

Cleveland Clinic. 2025d. "Emotional Dysregulation." Cleveland Clinic. https://my.clevelandclinic.org/health/symptoms/25065-emotional-dysregulation

Cleveland Clinic. 2025e. "Neurodivergent." Cleveland Clinic. https://my.clevelandclinic.org/health/symptoms/23154-neurodivergent

Coughlan, Maeve, and Helen Lynch. 2024. "'Can I Play Too?' A Qualitative Study of Outdoor Play and Participation among Autistic Preschoolers." *The American Journal of Occupational Therapy* 78(4). https://doi.org/10.5014/ajot.2024.050732

Coupé, Cynthia. 2023. "Neurodiversity as a Super Power." OARacle Newsletter. https://researchautism.org/oaracle-newsletter/neurodiversity-as-a-super-power/

Dabalsa, Jennifer M. 2017. "Dance for Special Needs Students: Building Confidence and Motor Skills." Masters thesis, University of Northern Colorado. https://digscholarship.unco.edu/theses/56

Dahlerbruch, Katie. 2022. "Proprioception: What Is It? (and 8 Signs of Dysfunction)." NAPA. https://napacenter.org/what-is-proprioception/

DeLussey, Stephanie. 2023. "What Is a Fidelity Check?" The Intentional IEP. https://www.theintentionaliep.com/fidelity-check/

Devi, G. 2022. "Classroom Aesthetics in Early Childhood Education." *International Journal of Early Childhood Special Education* 14(8): 3062–3069. DOI:10.48047/intjecse/V14I8.429

Dufault, Renee J., et al. 2023. "Higher Rates of Autism and Attention Deficit/Hyperactivity Disorder in American Children: Are Food Quality Issues Impacting Epigenetic Inheritance?" *World Journal of Clinical Pediatrics* 12(2): 25–37.

Edwards, Scott. 2015. "Dancing and The Brain." Harvard Medical School. https://hms.harvard.edu/news-events/publications-archive/brain/dancing-brain

EUNA Solutions. 2024. "What Is a Special Education Progress Monitoring Graph?" EUNA Solutions. https://eunasolutions.com/resources/what-is-a-special-education-progress-monitoring-graph/#:~:text=Progress%20monitoring%20graphs%20typically%20come,progress%20within%20special%20education%20programs

Fisher, Matthew. 2024. "Why It's Important to Create a Sensory-Friendly Classroom." Autism Parenting. https://www.autismparentingmagazine.com/important-create-sensory-friendly-classroom/

Forest School Association. n.d. "What Is Forest School?" Forest School Association. https://forestschoolassociation.org/what-is-forest-school/

Gallery, Erik. 2023. "A Guide on Self-Advocacy." Autism Alliance of Michigan. https://autismallianceofmichigan.org/a-guide-to-self-advocacy/

Garey, Juliann. 2024a. "The Controversy around ABA." Child Mind Institute. https://childmind.org/article/controversy-around-applied-behavior-analysis/

Garey, Juliann. 2024b. "The Power of Mindfulness." Child Mind Institute. https://childmind.org/article/the-power-of-mindfulness/

Gensic, Jennifer. 2015. "5 Tips for Teaching Autism Self-Advocacy." Learn from Autistic People. https://learnfromautistics.com/autism-self-advocacy-tips/

Gillette, Hope. 2023. "Why We No Longer Say High or Low Functioning for Autism." Healthline. https://www.healthline.com/health/autism/functioning-labels-autism

Giorgi, Anna. 2024. "Pet Therapy." Healthline. https://www.healthline.com/health/pet-therapy

Goodman, Brenda. 2023. "Sensory Processing Disorder." WebMD. https://www.webmd.com/children/sensory-processing-disorder

Goodman, Joshua, Michael Hurwitz, Jisung Park, and Jonathan Smith. 2018. "Heat and Learning." Working paper. National Bureau of Economic Research. https://www.nber.org/papers/w24639

Graaf, Genevieve, Philip Baiden, Latocia Keyes, and George Boyd. 2022. "Barriers to Mental Health Services for Parents and Siblings of Children with Special Health Care Needs." *Journal of Family Studies* 31(3): 881-895.

Hartman, Davida, et al. 2024. "What Does It Mean to Be Neurodiversity Affirmative?" The British Psychological Society. https://www.bps.org.uk/psychologist/what-does-it-mean-be-neurodiversity-affirmative

Harvard Health. 2017. "A Strengths-Based Approach to Autism." Harvard Health Publishing. https://www.health.harvard.edu/blog/a-strength-focused-approach-to-autism-2017042011607

IRIS Center. n.d. *Track Fidelity of Implementation.* https://iris.peabody.vanderbilt.edu/wp-content/uploads/modules/iep02/pdf/IRIS_track_fidelity_of_implementation.pdf

IRIS Center. 2025. "IEPs: How Administrators Can Support the Development and Implementation of High-Quality IEPs." IRIS Center. https://iris.peabody.vanderbilt.edu/module/iep02/cresource/q2/p06/

Institut National D'Etudes Demographiques. 2024. "2024: The United Nations Publishes New World Population Projections." INED. https://www.ined.fr/en/everything_about_population/demographic-facts-sheets/focus-on/2024-les-nations-unies-publient-de-nouvelles-projections-de-population-mondiale/#:~:text=world%20population%20projections-,2024%3A%20the%20United%20Nations%20publishes%20new%20world%20population%20projections,for%202050%20is%209.7%20billion

Irlen Diagnostic Clinics. 2025. "Irlen Syndrome." Irlen Diagnostic Clinics. https://irlenclinics.com.au/irlen-syndrome/

Joanna. 2023. "Childcare Classroom Design: 6 Factors that Impact the Children's Behavior." Childcare Renovation. https://www.childcarerenovation.com/childcare-classroom-design-impacts/

Johns Hopkins Medicine. 2025. "Art, Dance, and Music." Johns Hopkins Medicine. https://www.hopkinsmedicine.org/health/wellness-and-prevention/art-dance-and-music

Kamanetz, Anya, and Meribah Knight. 2020. "Schools Are Embracing Mindfulness, but Practice Doesn't Always Make Perfect." NPR. https://www.npr.org/2020/02/27/804971750/schools-are-embracing-mindfulness-but-practice-doesnt-always-make-perfect

Kamps, Louisa. 2023. "What Is Mindfulness? Why I Can Be Helpful for Children." Mayo Clinic. https://mcpress.mayoclinic.org/parenting/what-is-mindfulness-why-it-can-be-helpful-for-children/

Kapp, Steven K. 2020. *Autistic Community and the Neurodiversity Movement: Stories from the Frontline.* Springer Open Access. https://link.springer.com/book/10.1007/978-981-13-8437-0

Kazda, Luise, et al. 2021. "Overdiagnosis of Attention-Deficit/Hyperactivity Disorder in Children and Adolescents." *JAMA* 4(4): e215335. doi: 10.1001/jamanetworkopen.2021.5335

Klonowska, Kamilla, and Eric Z. Chen. 2024. "Meet the Demands of the Future Today with Universal Design for Learning." The Future of Education Conference, Florence, Italy. June 20–21. https://conference.pixel-online.net/library_scheda.php?id_abs=6514

Koukourikos, Konstantinos, Athanasia Georgopoulou, Lambrini Kourkouta, and Areti Tsaloglidou. 2019. "Benefits of Animal Assisted Therapy in Mental Health." *International Journal of Caring Sciences* 12(3): 1898–1905.

Krasnow, Donna, and Virginia Wilmerding. 2021. "Motor Development and the Young Dancer." The Dance Health Alliance of Canada, 2021.

Krauss, David. 2024. "Atypical Sensory Processing, Neurodivergence, and Autism." Psychology Today. https://www.psychologytoday.com/us/blog/atypical-children-extraordinary-parenting/202409/atypical-sensory-processing-neurodivergence

Laurie, Corinna. 2022. "Autistic Children and Motor Skills." National Autistic Society. https://www.autism.org.uk/advice-and-guidance/professional-practice/motor-skills-1

Legano, Lori A., et al. 2021. "Maltreatment of Children with Disabilities." *Pediatrics* 147(5): e2021050920. https://doi.org/10.1542/peds.2021-050920

Li, Donying, et al. 2019. "Exposure to Nature for Children with Autism Spectrum Disorder: Benefits, Caveats, and Barriers." *Health and Place* 55: 71–79. https://doi.org/10.1016/j.healthplace.2018.11.005

Linder, Jason N. 2019. "5 Ways Mindfulness Practice Positively Changes Your Brain." Psychology Today. https://www.psychologytoday.com/us/blog/mindfulness-insights/201905/5-ways-mindfulness-practice-positively-changes-your-brain

London Image Institute. 2020. "Color Psychology: How Do Colors Affect Mood and Emotions?" London Image Institute. https://londonimageinstitute.com/how-to-empower-yourself-with-color-psychology/

Madhan, Anagha. 2023. "The Dancing Brain—The Cognitive Effects of Dance." The Lewis Foundation of Classical Ballet, July 6, 2023.

Mann, Jeff, et al. 2022. "Getting out of the Classroom and into Nature: A Systematic Review of Nature-Specific Outdoor Learning on School Children's Learning and Development." *Frontiers in Public Health* 10. https://doi.org/10.3389/fpubh.2022.877058

Martinelli, Katherine. 2025. "Learning Disabilities and Self-Advocacy." Child Mind Institute. https://childmind.org/article/learning-disabilities-and-self-advocacy/

Maryville University. 2020. "Nature vs. Nurture Child Development: Exploring Key Differences." Maryville University. https://online.maryville.edu/blog/nature-vs-nurture-child-development/

Mastermind Behavior. 2024. "Examples of SMART Goals for Autism Students." Mastermind Behavior. https://www.mastermindbehavior.com/post/examples-of-smart-goals-students-autism

Maynard, Trisha. 2007. "Forest Schools in Great Britain: An Initial Exploration." *Contemporary Issues in Early Childhood* 8(4): 320–331.

Mayo Clinic. 2025a. "Autism Spectrum Disorder." Mayo Clinic. https://www.mayoclinic.org/diseases-conditions/autism-spectrum-disorder/symptoms-causes/syc-20352928

Mayo Clinic. 2025b. "Dyslexia." Mayo Clinic. https://www.mayoclinic.org/diseases-conditions/dyslexia/symptoms-causes/syc-20353552#:~:text=Dyslexia%20is%20a%20learning%20disorder,the%20brain%20that%20process%20language

Mayo Clinic. 2025c. "Epilepsy." Mayo Clinic. https://www.mayoclinic.org/diseases-conditions/epilepsy/symptoms-causes/syc-20350093

Mayo Clinic. 2025d. "Prader-Willi Syndrome." Mayo Clinic. https://www.mayoclinic.org/diseases-conditions/prader-willi-syndrome/symptoms-causes/syc-20355997

Mayo Clinic. 2025e. "Tourette Syndrome." Mayo Clinic. https://www.mayoclinic.org/diseases-conditions/tourette-syndrome/symptoms-causes/syc-20350465

McLeod, Saul. 2024. "Sensorimotor Stage of Cognitive Development." Simply Psychology. https://www.simplypsychology.org/sensorimotor.html

Montaser, Jamal, et al. 2023. "Correlations between the Development of Social Anxiety and Individuals with Autism Spectrum Disorder: A Systematic Review." *Cureus* 15(9): e44841. doi: 10.7759/cureus.44841

Morin, Amanda. 2024. "Classroom Accommodations for Sensory Processing Challenges." Understood. https://www.understood.org/en/articles/classroom-accommodations-for-sensory-processing-challenges

Moses, Amanda. 2023. "Why Has There Been a Rise in Autism and ADHD Diagnoses?" Psychology Today. https://www.psychologytoday.com/us/blog/thinking-about-becoming-a-psychologist/202307/why-has-there-been-a-rise-in-autism-and-adhd

Murphy, Lisa. 2024. "Understanding Vestibular Input and Its Role in Sensory Regulation." NAPA. https://napacenter.org/vestibular-input/

NASA Spinoff. 2019. "NASA Plant Research Offers a Breath of Fresh Air." NASA Spinoff. https://spinoff.nasa.gov/Spinoff2019/cg_7.html

National Autistic Society. 2020. "Sleep and Autism." National Autistic Society. https://www.autism.org.uk/advice-and-guidance/topics/physical-health/sleep

National Institute of Mental Health. n.d. "Social Anxiety Disorder: More Than Just Shyness." National Institute of Mental Health. https://www.nimh.nih.gov/health/publications/social-anxiety-disorder-more-than-just-shyness#:~:text=Social%20anxiety%20disorder%20is%20an,social%20anxiety%20disorder%20is%20treatable.

National Institute of Mental Health. 2025a. "Autism Spectrum Disorder." National Institute of Mental Health. https://www.nimh.nih.gov/health/topics/autism-spectrum-disorders-asd

National Institute of Mental Health. 2025b. "Bipolar Disorder." National Institute of Mental Health. https://www.nimh.nih.gov/health/topics/bipolar-disorder#:~:text=What%20is%20bipolar%20disorder%3F,day%2Dto%2Dday%20tasks.

National Institute of Mental Health. 2025c. "Obsessive-Compulsive Disorder (OCD)." National Institute of Mental Health. https://www.nimh.nih.gov/health/topics/obsessive-compulsive-disorder-ocd

National Institutes of Health. 2024. "Invisible Disabilities." NIH Style Guide. https://www.nih.gov/nih-style-guide/disabilities

National Recreation and Park Association. n.d. *Children in Nature: Improving Health by Reconnecting Youth with the Outdoors*. https://www.nrpa.org/uploadedFiles/nrpa.org/Advocacy/Children-in-Nature.pdf

Natural England. 2016. "England's Largest Outdoor Learning Project Reveals Children More Motivated to Learn when Outside." Gov.UK. https://www.gov.uk/government/news/englands-largest-outdoor-learning-project-reveals-children-more-motivated-to-learn-when-outside

OutClass. 2025. "Outdoor Classrooms: A Simple Definition." OutClass. https://outdoorclassrooms.com/blog/outdoor-classrooms-a-simple-definition/

Palumbo, Jennifer J. 2024. "How Companies Can Foster the Strengths of Neurodivergent Employees." Forbes. https://www.forbes.com/sites/jenniferpalumbo/2024/06/27/how-companies-can-foster-the-strengths-of-neurodivergent-employees/

Pandey, Ramendra P., et al. 2024. "The Role of Animal-Assisted Therapy in Enhancing Patients' Well-Being: Systematic Study of the Qualitative and Quantitative Evidence." *JMIRx Med*. 5: 51787. doi: 10.2196/51787

PBS. 1998. "Albert Einstein." A Science Odyssey: People and Discoveries. https://www.pbs.org/wgbh/aso/databank/entries/bpeins.html

Pillai, Rajapillai, and Jacqueline M. Branch. 2023. "IEPs and 504 Plans: A Guide for Parents." HealthyChildren.org. https://healthychildren.org/English/health-issues/conditions/developmental-disabilities/Pages/Individuulized Education-Program.aspx?gad_source=1&gbraid=0AAAADyMpZHEbDt70cq4Q5QVbISR58L14&gclid=CjwKCAiA65m7BhAwEiwAAgu4JAzZKm5TriCx5VoYAK4_IN38Me-B8QIHbZbBFP9Jc17wOf9ivETAWRoCECgQAvD_BwE

Post, Gail. 2022. "The Interface of Overthinking, Anxiety, and Shame among Gifted Children." SENG. https://www.sengifted.org/post/the-interface-of-overthinking-anxiety-and-shame-among-gifted-children

Powers, Richard. 2010. "Use It or Lose It: Dancing Makes You Smarter, Longer." Stanford University, July 30th, 2010.

Pritts, Mia. 2024. "Autism and Nature: Structured Outdoor Learning." Autism Parenting. https://www.autismparentingmagazine.com/nurture-structured-outdoor-learning/

Pryal, Katie R. G. 2024. "How Suspicion Feeds Stigma against Neurodivergent People." *Psychology Today.* https://www.psychologytoday.com/us/blog/living-neurodivergence/202311/how-suspicion-feeds-stigma-against-neurodivergent-people

Psychology Today. 2025. "Masking." *Psychology Today.* https://www.psychologytoday.com/us/basics/masking

Purba, Christopher A. P., Nining Febriyana, and Yunias Setiawati. 2024. "Managing Aggressive Behavior in Adolescents with Autism Spectrum Disorder: Pharmacological and Non-Pharmacological Approaches." *Journal of the Korean Academy of Child and Adolescent Psychiatry* 35(4): 223–229.

Raap, Edith, Katie L. Weille, and Christine Dedding. 2023. "'It's Up to Me Because I Gave Him This Life' How the Awareness of Being Permanently and Unconditionally Responsible Shapes the Experience of Chronic Sorrow in Parents of Disabled Children." *Psychology and Health* 1–21. doi:10.1080/08870446.2024.2378736.

Rabindran, Darshini M. 2020. "Piaget's Theory and Stages of Cognitive Development: An Overview." *Scholars Journal of Applied Medical Sciences* 8(9): 2152–2157.

Rathore, Mrithunjay, et al. 2023. "Functional Connectivity of Prefrontal Cortex in Various Meditation Techniques—A Mini-Review." *International Journal of Yoga* 15(3): 187–194. doi: 10.4103/ijoy.ijoy_88_22

Reggio Emilia Early Learning Centre. 2023. "The Reggio Emilia Approach: How Is It Different?" Reggio Emilia Early Learning Centre. https://reggioemilia.com.au/blog/the-reggio-emilia-approach-how-is-it-different/

Reznick, Ariane. 2023. "What Does It Mean to Be Neurodivergent?" Verywell Mind. https://www.verywellmind.com/what-is-neurodivergence-and-what-does-it-mean-to-be-neurodivergent-5196627

Ridderinkhof, Anna, Esther de Bruin, René Blom, and Susan M. Bögels. 2017. "Mindfulness-Based Program for Children with Autism Spectrum Disorder and Their Parents: Direct and Long-Term Improvements." *Mindfulness* 9(3): 773–791. doi: 10.1007/s12671-017-0815-x

Roberts, Julie. 2022. "Neurodiversity-Affirming Therapy: Positions, Therapy Goals, and Best Practices." Therapist Neurodiversity Collective. https://therapistndc.org/neurodiversity-affirming-therapy/

Roeloffs, Mary W. 2024. "Surgeon General Urges More Governmental Support for Parents Amid Mental Health Struggles." Forbes. https://www.forbes.com/sites/maryroeloffs/2024/08/28/surgeon-general-urges-more-governmental-support-for-parents-amid-mental-health-struggles/

Russell, Ginny. 2020. "Critiques of the Neurodiversity Movement." In *Autistic Community and the Neurodiversity Movement*. Springer Open Access. https://link.springer.com/chapter/10.1007/978-981-13-8437-0_21#citeas

Russell, Nicola. 2019. "The Importance of Environmental Aesthetics to Educator and Child Well-Being." The Sector. https://thesector.com.au/2019/05/20/the-importance-of-environmental-aesthetics-to-educator-and-child-wellbeing/

ScienceDirect. 2024. "Proprioception." ScienceDirect. https://www.sciencedirect.com/topics/neuroscience/proprioception

Sharman, Tamara. 2022. "What Is Interoception? The '8th Sense' Explained." NAPA. https://napacenter.org/interoception/

Siever, Larry J. 2008. "Neurobiology of Aggression and Violence." *American Journal of Psychiatry* 165(4): 429–442. doi: 10.1176/appi.ajp.2008.07111774

Sirven, Joseph I., and Patty O. Shafer. 2014. "Related Conditions." Epilepsy Foundation. https://www.epilepsy.com/parents-and-caregivers/talking-kids-about-epilepsy/related-conditions

Soldovieri, Antonia. 2024. "Thinking, Talking, Teaching: How Primary School Educators Facilitate Neurodiversity-Affirming Classroom Practices to Support Students' Inclusion." Thesis, University of British Columbia. DOI 10.14288/1.0447762

Stearns, Kaitlynn. 2022. "Creating a Sensory Friendly Classroom." Occupational Therapy Capstones 531. University of North Dakota. https://commons.und.edu/ot-grad/531

Stone, Alyssa. n.d. "Harnessing the Power of Music Therapy for Neurodivergent Children: A Guide for Parents." CAYR Connections. https://www.cayrconnections.org/post/harnessing-the-power-of-music-therapy-for-neurodivergent-children-a-guide-for-parents#:~:text=Music%20therapy%20is%20a%20powerful,goals%20within%20a%20therapeutic%20relationship.

Swain, Kristine D., Jessica L. Hagaman, and Elizabeth M. Leader-Janssen. 2021. "Teacher-Reported IEP Goal Data Collection Methods." *Preventing School Failure: Alternative Education for Children and Youth* 66(2): 118–125.

Terada, Youki, and Stephen Merrill. 2023. "The Science of Classroom Design." Edutopia. https://www.edutopia.org/article/the-science-of-classroom-design/

Uherek-Bradecka, Barbara. 2020. "Classroom Design for Children with an Autism Spectrum." IOP Conference Series: Material Science and Engineering 960. 5th World Multidisciplinary Civil Engineering-Architecture-Urban Planning Symposium. Prague, Czech Republic. DOI 10.1088/1757-899X/960/2/022100

University College London. 2019. "Spending Time in Nature Can Improve Children's Confidence." UCL News. https://www.ucl.ac.uk/news/2019/nov/spending-time-nature-can-improve-childrens-confidence

UPMC Health Beat. 2014. "How Music Affects a Child's Brain." UPMC Health Beat. https://share.upmc.com/2014/12/how-music-affects-a-childs-brain/

University of Rochester Medical Center. 2025. "Understanding Autism: What It Is and What It Isn't." University of Rochester Medical Center. https://www.urmc.rochester.edu/news/publications/health-matters/what-is-autism

US Department of Education. 2024. "A History of the Individuals with Disabilities Education Act." IDEA. https://sites.ed.gov/idea/IDEA-History

US Department of Education. 2025. "IDEA: Individuals with Disabilities Education Act." US Department of Education. https://sites.ed.gov/idea/

Velkoff, David F. 2025. "What Is Stimming in Autism?" Drake Institute of Neurophysical Medicine. https://www.drakeinstitute.com/what-is-stimming-in-autism

Vromen, Joyce. 2023. "A Strengths-Based Approach to Neurodiversity." Psychology Today. https://www.psychologytoday.com/us/blog/divergent-minds/202301/a-strengths-based-approach-to-neurodiversity

Ward, William A. 2009. "Curiosity Is the Wick in the Candle of Learning." Penn State Extension. https://extension.psu.edu/programs/betterkidcare/parents-families/families-count/curiosity-is-the-wick-in-the-candle-of-learning

Wedge, Marilyn. 2018. "7 Ways Mindfulness Can Help Children's Brains." Psychology Today. https://www.psychologytoday.com/us/blog/suffer-the-children/201809/7-ways-mindfulness-can-help-children-s-brains

Wideman-van der Laan, Ymkje. 2023. "The Critical Role of Visual Design in K–12 Classrooms." EDSpaces. https://ed-spaces.com/stories/the-critical-role-of-visual-design-in-k-12-classrooms/

Williams, Dilafruz, and P. Scott Dixon. 2013. "Impact of Garden-Based Learning on Academic Outcomes in Schools: Synthesis of Research between 1990 and 2010." *American Educational Research Association* 83(2): 211–235.

Woolridge, Shannon. 2023. "Writing Respectfully: Person-First and Identity-First Language." National Institutes of Health. https://www.nih.gov/about-nih/what-we-do/science-health-public-trust/perspectives/writing-respectfully-person-first-identity-first-language

Worth, Karen. 2010. "Science in Early Childhood Classrooms: Content and Process." Early Childhood Research and Practice. https://ecrp.illinois.edu/beyond/seed/worth.html

Zauderer, Steven. 2023. "Art Therapy and Autism: Empowering Expression." Cross River Therapy. https://www.crossrivertherapy.com/autism/art-therapy-and-autism#goals-and-objectives-of-art-therapy-for-autism

INDEX

NUMBERS

A

B

C

D

N

O

P

Q

R

S

T

U

V

W

Y